AMERICA'S MOST ICONIC ICE CREAMS

Tyler Malek and JJ Goode

Photographs by Stephanie Shih

CLARKSON POTTER/PUBLISHERS
NEW YORK

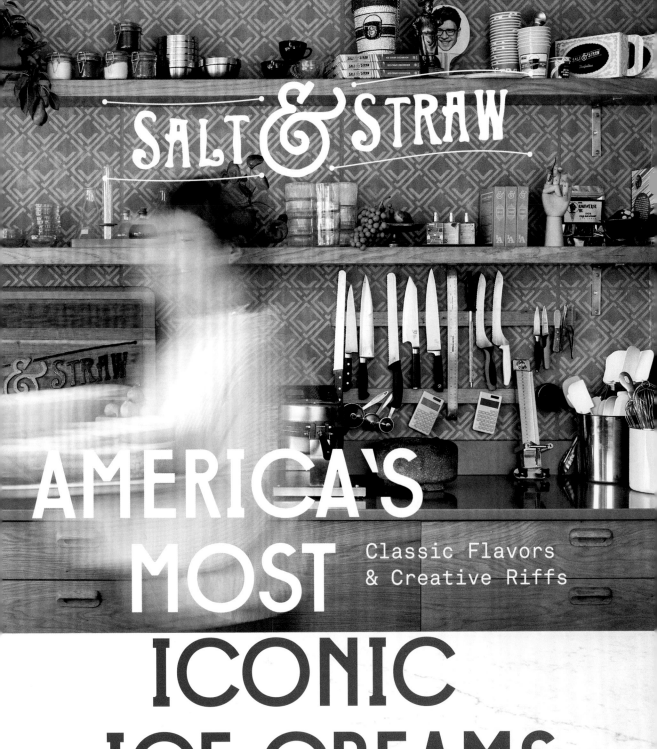

SALT & STRAW

AMERICA'S MOST ICONIC ICE CREAMS

Classic Flavors & Creative Riffs

CONTENTS

HOW THE FLAVOR JOURNEY BEGAN • 7

WHAT THIS BOOK IS ALL ABOUT • 10

WHAT YOU NEED TO MAKE GREAT ICE CREAMS • 13

THE BASE RECIPES 18

VANILLA 28

CHOCOLATE 54

COFFEE 104

STRAWBERRY 84

COOKIE DOUGH 126

SALTED CARAMEL 152

PISTACHIO 180

CEREAL 206

GREEN TEA 214

RUM RAISIN 234

ACKNOWLEDGMENTS • 251
INDEX • 252

HOW THE FLAVOR JOURNEY BEGAN

Long before Salt & Straw was the biggest small-batch ice cream company in the world, it was just twenty-three-year-old me, my brilliant cousin Kim, and an erratic freezer in Portland, Oregon. Then a cup of coffee changed everything.

I had just quit my job as the world's kindest and least effective car salesman (don't ask) and convinced Kim to consider me for the position of head ice cream maker for the shop she planned to open in Portland. Minor detail: I had never made ice cream in my entire life. So an hour later, I walked into a Goodwill in Seattle, bought four $4 ice cream makers, and started experimenting. After a week of maxing out the machines, I had recipes for thirty flavors and sent them to Kim. Because of (or perhaps despite) the unlikely inspirations I dreamt up—grapefruit with sage, coffee with bone marrow—she agreed to give me a shot.

    I moved into Kim's basement and enrolled part time in culinary school. I figured maybe I should know something about making food before I got into the business of, well, making food. In the morning, I attended classes. In the afternoon, I went to a commissary kitchen to test out flavors for our fledgling ice cream operation. And on the way to the latter, I'd take my notebook to a coffee shop for a cup and a think.

This was Portland in 2011, so that shop happened to be Stumptown Coffee's The Annex. Back then, Stumptown wasn't yet a household name and an emblem of direct-trade and culinary artisanship. It was still just a neo-punk outfit making waves for its revolutionary sourcing practices and exceptional coffee. Or at least, what I'd heard was exceptional coffee. At the time, I didn't know good coffee from the Folgers crystals my culinary school professor used to make tiramisu.

In your wildest, most *Portlandia*-inflected dreams, you couldn't have imagined the scene at The Annex. Behind the counter was a small army of baristas, their long mustaches waxed, their bodies covered in flash tattoos. The menu on the wall listed no dark roasts or Frappuccinos but eighteen single-origin coffees and six brewing techniques, including but not limited to those enabled by the Seussian contraptions—multichambered glass beakers, squiggly tubes, and the like—on display. When you approached the counter to order, you'd get a long spiel about the various beans and then another about the pros and cons of the different brewing techniques. Fifteen minutes later, you'd have a cup of coffee. The process was ludicrous, condescending, and impractical. I absolutely loved it.

The height of absurdity came when I stumbled upon a cupping. When a novel bean arrived at The Annex, meticulously sourced and locally roasted, the baristas would have a formal tasting (a cupping, in coffee-industry parlance) and invite anyone in the shop to participate. Baby-faced and still in my checkered culinary school pants, I lined up behind the city's bewhiskered baristas and Third Wave coffee geeks, trying to memorize the ritual I watched them perform—pour, wait, crack, skim—before they had their first tastes, each one punctuated by an ostentatiously loud slurp.

Then I listened as they discussed the flavors of the different coffees. The existence of those two plurals blew my mind. First, I hadn't known there were *coffees*—thousands upon thousands of varieties of plants that produce the fruit that gives us coffee beans. Second, I didn't realize coffee had *flavors*. To be honest, I thought coffee *was* a flavor—a single bitter, vaguely chocolatey profile. How wrong I was.

Over the course of a year, I tasted more than one hundred different coffee beans, many of them brewed in multiple ways. By the end, simply ordering a cup of coffee seemed as silly as going to a restaurant and asking for a glass of grape wine. I learned that I loved Guatemalan El Injerto brewed as a pour-over and served with a dash of simple syrup to play up its notes of cherry. That Indonesian Gajah Aceh brewed as espresso was my personal favorite, its intense chocolatey flavor tinged with blackberry and tobacco heightened with a generous splash of cream and two big spoonfuls of sugar.

It's hard to explain how profoundly this experience affected me. I quit school. I scrapped those first thirty flavors, which I'd scribbled down while sipping a caffè latte at a Seattle Starbucks. I began to let curiosity be my guide. Suddenly, every ingredient, every basic, familiar pleasure seemed to have secret potential, its own universe that I had never imagined. If I had been in the dark about coffee, even as a student in culinary school who was supposed to be learning about food, what else was I missing?

So, so much, it turns out. Once I knew to look, I found revelation everywhere. I sampled salt crystals of various shapes, colors, sizes, and flavors with Mark Bitterman, author of a manifesto on the delectable mineral. I discussed orchid pollination with Bill and Marty of Singing Dog, the Stumptown Coffee of Papua New Guinea–grown vanilla beans. Suddenly, I felt like I was looking through a powerful telescope after years of standard sky-gazing: each ingredient, once a single faint star, was now revealed to be a brilliant constellation.

And it made a huge difference in my ice cream making. Just as they do for cooking, great ingredients massively upgrade your frozen treats. But for me, learning about the particulars of coffee and chocolate, vanilla and spirits, nuts and tea from various local artisans and gurus ultimately did more than just elevate the ice creams I wanted to make. It inspired them. Before my Stumptown conversion, for example, I might have set out to make a great coffee ice cream. But now that I knew coffee was an entire galaxy and not a single planet, I began to hobnob with roasters, baristas, and coffee growers and ultimately designed coffee ice creams (more than twenty to date) in order to showcase the qualities unique to each bean. The more I learned about ingredients, the better my ice cream became.

WHAT THIS BOOK IS ALL ABOUT

Since Salt & Straw began, we have been devoted to celebrating great ingredients in frozen form. Yet for the life of our shops, we've always avoided one thing: making the classics. I'm talking about chocolate, coffee, rum raisin—all of the absolutely delicious flavors you see at ice cream parlors around the country. That is, until now.

I've always felt that nostalgia is an unbeatable competitor—why would you take on the iconic, nostalgia-laden scoops that define that kid-at-an-ice-cream-stand feeling? Well, pondering the importance and intricacy of ingredients recently got me thinking about why those classics became classics in the first place. What if understanding those ingredients could help us not reinvent the classics but exalt them?

So, in this book, we will finally share the epic Salt & Straw version of ten of the country's most famous flavors, applying our deep affection for the anchoring ingredients and our mastery of ice cream science to make mind-blowing renditions that stay true to their archetypes. That means vanilla ice cream that showcases the incredible complex flavors of the dried cured seedpod

of a climbing orchid we know as vanilla. That means coffee ice cream that reveals the galaxy of flavors that result from careful growing, processing, and brewing. That means chocolate ice cream that shares that pleasure of indulging in a quality chocolate bar, and rum raisin that reinvigorates the stodgy scoop with top-shelf dark rum and plump fruit. After sharing the classic, we'll blast off in five or so different directions with recipes that apply the delicious logic behind the classic. It's still Salt & Straw, after all.

Along with the recipes, we'll share some (geeky) details about their muse—be it chocolate or coffee, green tea or pistachio. Because even a little new knowledge goes a long way toward improving your ice cream and inspiring new adventures. Some of you might skip my ramblings about butterfat percentages and ice crystal formation and just follow the recipes. And you'll be thrilled, because the results will be insanely delicious.

Following these recipes will guide you to our hard-won flavors, but I want you to know that carving your own path is not just okay but recommended. Because ice cream should be fun—and let's be honest, when you start with good ingredients, add cream and sugar, then churn it, it's going to be delicious, no matter how badly you screw up. If it's frozen, it's ice cream. If it's not, pour it over some cake, because yum.

WHAT YOU NEED TO MAKE GREAT ICE CREAMS

NOTE · ALL THE ICE CREAMS IN THIS BOOK WERE DEVELOPED FOR MACHINES WITH A 1½-QUART CAPACITY.

ICE CREAM MACHINES

To make ice cream, you'll need an ice cream machine. The good news is they're not expensive, though you can certainly splurge if you choose, and they'll all work well for the purposes of this book. Here are the three main types:

HAND-CRANK

While electric machines abound, you can still successfully use this low-tech device to make delicious ice cream. The only downside is that you have to turn a crank to power the churning, which to some of us counts as an upside—it's fun! Bonus: The machines churn ice cream in nearly half the time it takes an electric machine.

FROZEN-BOWL

These are electric machines that rely on a bowl filled with coolant to freeze your ice cream as it churns. They're great, easy to use, and affordable. The downside is that before churning, you must freeze the bowl for 24 hours (and between batches of ice cream, for another 12 to 24 hours). For anyone with a small freezer or a hankering to make multiple flavors in a day, this is sub-ideal. Note: For best results, make sure the ice cream base is very cold—six hours in the fridge should do it. For the fastidious among you, you're shooting for 40°F or below.

INTERNAL COMPRESSOR

These are your priciest option, but because they operate with compressors that create their own cold—just like your freezer—you don't have to prefreeze a bowl before (or between) batches or make sure your ice cream mixture is super-cold before churning. Machines with particularly strong compressors churn faster, which means less air and better butterfat structure. So ask yourself whether slightly better ice cream is worth the price.

FREEZING & STORAGE

Once you've churned your ice cream, it's time to turn it into the treat of your dreams by popping it in the freezer. The ice cream goes from 25°F and soft to about 10°F and the solidly scoopable texture we all know and love. To do this right, and thereby retain as many of the teeny tiny ice crystals that make up good ice cream, you want to get the ice cream as cold as you can right after it's churned. Wait too long and those little crystals will melt and then refreeze into bigger crystals (at this point, not even xanthan gum can save you!). The bigger the crystals, the more likely you are to sense them when you lick, and the less lovely the ice cream will be. With that in mind, here are your post-churning priorities.

● A few hours before you make ice cream, reduce your freezer's temperature, if you're able.

● After it's churned, immediately transfer the ice cream to containers (see page 17). If you're adding mix-ins, do so quickly.

● Before covering with a lid, press a small sheet of parchment paper against the ice cream to protect the surface from warm air that could collect beneath the lid. It's okay if the parchment hangs over the rim.

● Store the ice cream near the back of your freezer (aka the coldest part), since it's farthest from the relatively warm air that rushes in when you open the door. And don't pack it in so it's butting against other stuff. Flowing cold air is what cools down the ice cream.

● And if you're feeling extra, line up some bodyguards of expendable items (sorry, frozen peas and lesser ice creams) to shield your precious pints from the warm air outside the freezer.

HOW TO SERVE YOUR ICE CREAM

When you're storing ice cream, the rule is: the colder the better. Our industrial freezers keep our ice creams at –20°F, at which temperature they'll basically last forever with no degradation in quality. But serving at that temperature, or even 0°F, the temperature of a home freezer, does not make for pleasant eating. Not only would the ice cream be rock hard, it would also take too long to melt on your tongue and release its deliciousness. That's why so many of us leave our pints and gallons on the counter until they soften. And you know what, that's just fine.

The thing is, at our shops we put so much care into our scoops, we want you to experience them at their best. We use high-tech refrigeration to dial in the ideal serving temperature for each variety of frozen treat: 5°F for ice cream and custard, 8°F for sherbets and sorbets, and 15°F for gelato. That's one reason gelato is so great for delicate flavors like strawberry—the main flavor receptors on your tongue work best at slightly warmer temperatures.

Now, these are all suggested temperatures. As a kid, I used to prefer my ice cream half melted, and any frozen treat made with dairy or coconut cream is delicious like this. Sorbet, however, has a smaller temperature window: Without the protein structure created by fat, it becomes sticky and unappealing when melted. Still, you do you!

STEP 1: Only remove the pints that you're going to eat—and eat every last bit. The reason is that once you bring your ice cream to tasty temperatures, refreezing it guarantees heat shock, aka those larger ice crystals that are one mark of a meh scoop. In other words, you *have* to eat it all now—for the good of the ice cream!

STEP 2: Bring it to temperature. You have three options. (1) Leave the pint on the counter, which totally works for the edges of the ice cream but not the center, which will stay unscoopably hard for a while longer. (2) Microwave in 5-second increments. I've found this tempers the ice cream more evenly. Or (3) If you've got the time, stick the ice cream in your fridge until it comes to temperature, 30 to 40 minutes—the best way, if you ask me.

STEP 3: Scoop! As soon as you can make nice round scoops, it's ready.

Dip your scoop—a plain old aluminum scoop (the Zeroll brand makes my fave)—in cold water, shake it dry, then drag it along the surface of the ice cream, starting at the opposite end and pulling toward yourself. Do this two or three times for each "scoop"—which, if you're wondering, will be gloriously round with small "ears" from the scoop's edges and slight "barking" (we call it that because it's a little craggy, like tree bark). Gelato is so soft that it's often smeared with a spoon or spade, but a trigger-scoop can give you pretty orbs if that's what you're after.

PARCHMENT PAPER

Whenever I make ice cream at home, I press a piece of parchment paper against the surface of the ice cream, just as you'd press plastic wrap against the top of pudding to prevent a skin from forming, before covering with the lid. This prevents ice crystals from forming on the surface, which isn't a huge deal but is a bit of a bummer. Don't have parchment? Add the lid, flip the container upside down, and freeze it that way.

CONTAINERS

I like using plastic pint or quart containers (the kind your takeout often comes in) or metal containers (less common, but boy do they help freeze your ice cream quickly, especially if you prechill them). I don't use glass because it can break at low temperatures. Because ice cream expands slightly as it freezes, be sure to leave a little space at the top.

STICK BLENDER

I love my stick blender. It's slim and trim, plus it's more effective than bulky countertop blenders at blending the kind of low-volume mixtures you need to make ice cream at home.

SILICONE BAKING MATS

Parchment paper and foil are just fine, but nothing beats a silicone baking mat when it comes to making or baking lovely sticky mix-ins like toffee and brittle.

CANDY THERMOMETER

A candy thermometer (preferably an instant-read digital one) is a must for making confections like fluffs and caramels. PS: Deep-fryers, rejoice—your thermometer is not just for candy but great for clocking oil temperature, too.

KOSHER SALT Every recipe in this book was developed and tested with Diamond Crystal brand kosher salt. This is important to mention because the same volume of the other most common brand, Morton, delivers nearly twice the saltiness. So if you opt for Morton, use about two-thirds the amount I call for.

THE BASE

GELATO BASE

ICE CREAM BASE

CUSTARD BASE

RECIPES

SORBET BASE

COCONUT BASE

What stock is to soup, bases are to ice cream.
Yet unlike slowly simmered stocks, bases take
mere minutes to make and give you the foundation
for every creamy frozen treat in this book—plus
an infinite number you can create yourself.

For the home cook, carving out a separate
recipe for the base has a different purpose.
It's practical and makes homemade ice cream that
much easier. You can make your bases in advance—
like stock, in big batches—keep them in the
freezer, and thaw when you're ready to flavor
and spin them into ice cream.

SALT & STRAW'S COVETED
17% BUTTERFAT BASE 22

THE RICHEST CUSTARD
BASE EVER 24

SALT & STRAW'S SUPER-DENSE
GELATO BASE 25

SALT & STRAW'S SUPER-EASY
SORBET/SHERBET BASE 26

SALT & STRAW'S VEGAN
COCONUT BASE 27

SALT & STRAW'S COVETED 17% BUTTERFAT BASE

This base is devised to max out your scoop's butterfat content. Any more and you'd be churning butter, not ice cream. Of course, we'll occasionally dilute this base on purpose—depending on your intention, high fat isn't always ideal—but when we want that iconic texture, the lush creaminess and fluffiness of proper ice cream, we maintain the ratios of this carefully calibrated concoction. Nerds, take note: Those ratios are approximately 58% water, 17% fat, 11% milk solids, and 14% sugar, by weight.

MAKES ABOUT
3 CUPS

½ cup granulated sugar

2 tablespoons nonfat dry milk powder

¼ teaspoon xanthan gum (yes, I'm easy to find!)

1⅓ cups whole milk

2 tablespoons light corn syrup

1⅓ cups heavy cream, very cold

In a small bowl, stir together the sugar, milk powder, and xanthan gum.

In a medium pot, stir together the whole milk and corn syrup. Add the sugar mixture and immediately whisk vigorously until smooth. Set the pot over medium heat and cook, stirring often and reducing the heat if necessary to prevent a simmer, just until the sugar has fully dissolved, about 3 minutes. Remove the pot from the heat. Add the cold cream and stir until fully combined.

Transfer the mixture to an airtight container and refrigerate until well chilled, at least 6 hours, or for even better texture and flavor, 24 hours. Stir well before using.

The base can be further stored in the fridge for up to 1 week or in the freezer for up to 3 months. Thaw completely and stir well before using.

MEET ICE CREAM'S BESTIE: XANTHAN GUM

Every recipe in this book uses xanthan gum in its base. Now, I know what you're thinking. It sounds funny! It must be impossible to find, not to mention evil! Well, it's not and it's not. It's available at the supermarket under ubiquitous brands like Bob's Red Mill and Hodgson Mill, and it's as innocuous as cornstarch or baking soda. In ice cream, xanthan gum combats "heat shock," the industry term for what happens when ice cream melts and then freezes again into bigger crystals—and the enemy of yummy ice cream. Because homemade ice cream lacks the controls of a high-tech ice cream operation, it's particularly susceptible to heat shock and therefore particularly welcoming of a little xanthan gum. Often used as a thickening agent, xanthan gum attracts and binds to water. If you use just enough, you get insurance against ice crystal growth at no cost to ice cream quality.

THE RICHEST CUSTARD BASE EVER

**MAKES ABOUT
3 CUPS**

½ cup granulated sugar

1 tablespoon nonfat
dry milk powder

⅛ teaspoon xanthan gum
(yes, I'm easy to find!)

1¼ cups whole milk

2 tablespoons light
corn syrup

6 large egg yolks

1 cup heavy cream,
very cold

We designed this base to re-create the divine pleasures of the frozen custard popular in the Midwest—softer than ice cream, harder than soft serve, and richer than both. The yolks add flavor and fat, allowing us to exceed the upper limit of butterfat. The dense foundation takes so well to what I think of as bakery flavors—roasted fruit, warm spices like nutmeg and allspice, chocolate, and vanilla. Because we really pack in the egg yolks to achieve the glorious texture you'd find at a Wisconsin mom-and-pop shop, each spoonful feels like a bite of super-cold crème brûlée.

In a small bowl, stir together the sugar, milk powder, and xanthan gum.

In a medium pot, stir together the whole milk and corn syrup. Add the sugar mixture and egg yolks and whisk vigorously until smooth. Set the pot over medium-low heat and stir constantly with a silicone spatula until the mixture steams, reducing the heat if necessary to prevent a simmer. Cook, stirring frequently, until the mixture thickens enough to coat the spatula, 5 to 7 minutes. Remove the pot from the heat.

Add the cold cream and stir well. Transfer the mixture to an airtight container and refrigerate until well chilled, at least 6 hours, or for even better texture and flavor, 24 hours. Stir well before using.

The base can be further stored in the fridge for up to 1 week or in the freezer for up to 3 months. Thaw completely and stir well before using.

SALT & STRAW'S SUPER-DENSE GELATO BASE

MAKES ABOUT 3 CUPS

⅔ cup granulated sugar

½ cup nonfat dry milk powder

¼ teaspoon xanthan gum (yes, I'm easy to find!)

2 cups whole milk

¼ cup light corn syrup

¼ cup heavy cream, very cold

As you well know, gelato isn't just the Italian version of ice cream. It's a different product altogether, with about half the fat and a much denser texture (less fat = less air after churning). The lower fat and air content are why flavors taste so vivid. This base is dialed in for all your gelato-making needs.

In a small bowl, stir together the sugar, milk powder, and xanthan gum.

In a medium pot, stir together the whole milk and corn syrup. Add the sugar mixture and immediately whisk vigorously until smooth. Set the pot over medium heat and cook, stirring often and reducing the heat if necessary to prevent a simmer, just until the sugar has fully dissolved, about 3 minutes. Remove the pot from the heat. Add the cold cream and stir until fully combined.

Transfer the mixture to an airtight container and refrigerate until well chilled, at least 6 hours, or for even better texture and flavor, 24 hours. Stir well before using.

The base can be further stored in the fridge for up to 1 week or in the freezer for up to 3 months. Thaw completely and stir well before using.

SALT & STRAW'S SUPER-EASY SORBET/ SHERBET BASE

MAKES ABOUT
2¾ CUPS

1½ cups granulated sugar

¾ teaspoon xanthan gum
    (yes, I'm easy to find!)

¼ cup plus
    2 tablespoons light
    corn syrup

The perfect sorbet is a carefully choreographed dance of sugar and water, with the sugar inhibiting the freezing of the water so the ice crystals grow at just the right pace. The result is a dense (no fat = minimal air) and velvety texture that conveys intense flavor (no fat to dull the palate) and then disappears (no fat to hold the flavor). The only way to get that flavor back is to take another lick.

Add a little dairy to this base, and you get sorbet's cousin, sherbet, which is still dense and intense in flavor but with a touch of creaminess.

In a small bowl, stir together the sugar and xanthan gum.

In a small saucepan, stir together 1½ cups water and the corn syrup. Add the sugar mixture and immediately whisk vigorously until well combined and mostly smooth. Set the pot over medium heat and cook, stirring often and adjusting the heat if necessary to prevent a simmer, until the sugar has fully dissolved, about 3 minutes. Take the pan off the heat and let cool to room temperature.

Transfer the mixture to an airtight container and refrigerate until well chilled, at least 4 hours.

At this point, you can keep it in the fridge for up to 2 weeks or in the freezer for up to 1 year. Thaw completely and stir well before using.

SALT & STRAW'S VEGAN COCONUT BASE

**MAKES ABOUT
3 CUPS**

- ½ cup granulated sugar
- ¼ teaspoon xanthan gum (yes, I'm easy to find!)
- ¼ cup light corn syrup
- 2 cups unsweetened coconut cream, chilled

Vegans and the dairy-sensitive shouldn't be given a life sentence of sorbet. Thanks to the very special fat of the coconut, everyone can enjoy the fluffy, creamy joys of proper ice cream as well as those of dense, satiny gelato and sherbet.

In a small bowl, stir together the sugar and xanthan gum.

In a medium pot, stir together ¾ cup water and the corn syrup. Add the sugar mixture and immediately whisk vigorously until smooth. Set the pot over medium heat and cook, stirring often and reducing the heat if necessary to prevent a simmer, just until the sugar has fully dissolved, about 3 minutes. Remove the pot from the heat. Add the chilled coconut cream and stir until fully combined.

Transfer the mixture to an airtight container and refrigerate until well chilled, at least 6 hours, or for even better texture and flavor, 24 hours. Stir well before using.

The base can be further stored in the fridge for up to 1 week or in the freezer for up to 3 months. Thaw completely and stir well before using.

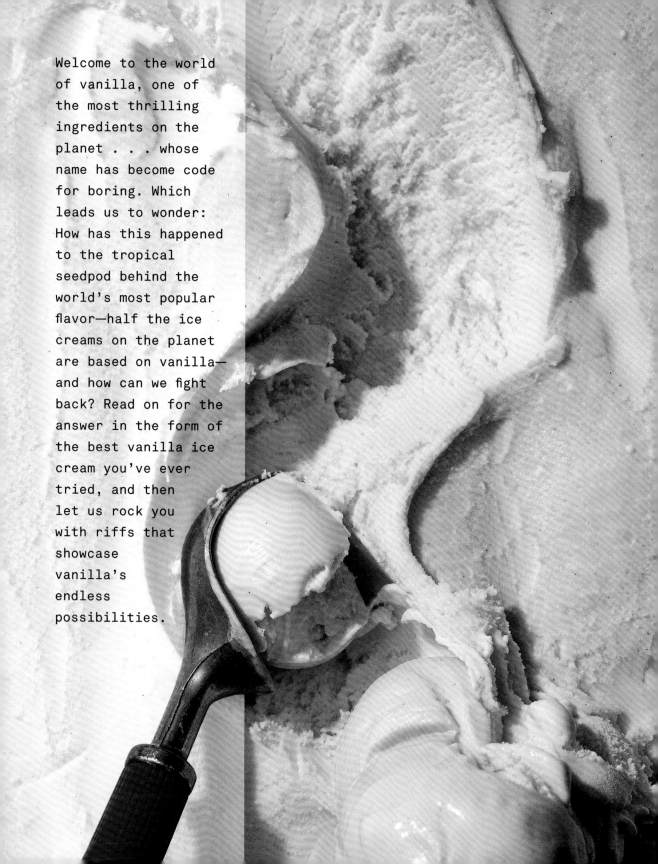

Welcome to the world of vanilla, one of the most thrilling ingredients on the planet . . . whose name has become code for boring. Which leads us to wonder: How has this happened to the tropical seedpod behind the world's most popular flavor—half the ice creams on the planet are based on vanilla—and how can we fight back? Read on for the answer in the form of the best vanilla ice cream you've ever tried, and then let us rock you with riffs that showcase vanilla's endless possibilities.

FRENCH VANILLA 32

BOURBON BROWN SUGAR VANILLA 38

VANILLA WITH CARAMELIZED
WHITE CHOCOLATE 38

HONEY-ROASTED BANANA VANILLA 39

SMOKED-CHERRY VANILLA 40

VANILLA CUSTARD WITH
BUTTERSCOTCH SWIRLS 42

BIRTHDAY CAKE & BLACKBERRIES 45

PASSION FRUIT VANILLA WITH
EXTRA-DARK CHOCOLATE FUDGE (V) 47

VANILLA WITH STICKY CROISSANTS
AND CARAMEL SWIRLS 50

VANILLA POACHED PEACH GELATO 53

OUR ULTIMATE

FRENCH VANILLA

MAKES ABOUT
2 PINTS

3   cups Rich Custard Base (page 24)

1½ teaspoons pure vanilla extract

1   teaspoon dark molasses (not blackstrap)

⅛ teaspoon Diamond Crystal kosher salt

1   vanilla bean

While Salt & Straw superfans come to our shops for cult classics like Goat Cheese Marionberry Habanero or Strawberry Honey Balsamic with Black Pepper, we do get the occasional customer who ignores his family's pleas to be adventurous and insists on getting vanilla. The groans! The eye rolls! Shh! Can I tell you something? Whenever I visit an ice cream shop that I'm excited to try, I do exactly the same thing! I order the vanilla.

Though it has become synonymous with dull, vanilla is one of the most incredible foodstuffs I've ever worked with. Its flavor is impossibly complex, composed of more than 220 chemical compounds. When someone opens a fine vanilla pod within a ten-foot radius, the aroma will inhabit your body, entering through your nose, hugging your soul, and then exiting from the nape of your neck like a cartoon ghost.

And while vanilla has countless uses in the sweet kitchen, when you want to truly *celebrate* top-notch vanilla beans, you've got to make ice cream. With your palate primed by sugar (which stimulates your taste receptors, telling your brain to "start tasting"), and the vanilla's arrival tantalizingly delayed by cold and fat (the cold dazes your taste buds, the fat slows the release of flavor), it arrives at last in a crescendo (fat intensifies vanilla's flavor, too)—all 220 compounds flooding your tongue in a sort of gastronomic slo-mo.

As a big vanilla booster, I've gone all out to create what I think is the ultimate version of the iconic scoop. The goal is to maximize the impact of the vanilla. So while I look to vanilla beans to provide those tempting specks, the major infusion of flavor comes from vanilla extract—the steeping process really opens up vanilla's complex flavors. And I suggest seeking out an excellent blended vanilla extract or mixing up your own (see Note), then using a touch of salt and molasses to play up vanilla's darker, savory side. The "French" part in the ice cream name is a nod to the addition of egg yolks in the base, which gives this ice cream a nostalgic yellow hue and, more important, helps the vanilla flavor enrobe your palate.

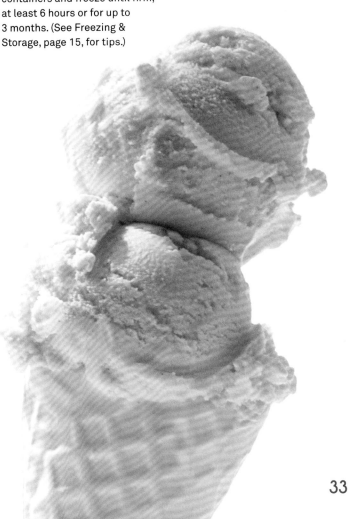

NOTE · IF YOU REALLY
WANT TO GO THE EXTRA
MILE, LOOK TO BLENDED
EXTRACTS, WHICH
DELIVER AN ESPECIALLY
COMPLEX AND BALANCED
VANILLA-Y-NESS AND
WHICH GOOD VANILLA
COMPANIES OFFER WITH
THE PRIDE OF VINTNERS
WHO MAKE FINE CHIANTI.
YOU CAN EVEN MIX
ONE UP YOURSELF.
MY FAVORITE: 1 PART
MEXICAN VANILLA,
2 PARTS BOURBON
VANILLA, AND 2 PARTS
TAHITIAN VANILLA.

In a medium bowl, combine the custard base, vanilla extract, molasses, and salt. Use the tip of a sharp knife to split the vanilla bean lengthwise. Use the knife to scrape the vanilla seeds into the bowl and stir well.

Pour the mixture into an ice cream maker and turn on the machine. Churn just until it has the texture of soft serve ice cream, 30 to 40 minutes, depending on the machine.

Transfer to freezer-safe containers and freeze until firm, at least 6 hours or for up to 3 months. (See Freezing & Storage, page 15, for tips.)

THE REAL THING

It's entirely possible that many vanilla lovers and haters—including me for the first twenty-three years of my life!—have *never actually tasted real vanilla*. Pound for pound, true vanilla is as valuable as silver, the most expensive of any spice save saffron. And so artificial vanilla abounds. Nearly half of the ice cream made in the United States (about 500 million gallons) is vanilla-based, much of it made with synthetic vanillin, a lab-made extract of just *one* of the *220-plus* flavor compounds in a vanilla bean. No wonder the notion of vanilla is such a snore.

The vanilla bean is the dried seedpod of a climbing orchid. It owes its place as one of the world's most precious spices to nature, the brutality of imperialism, and the ingenuity of a twelve-year-old kid. Vanilla was cultivated as medicine by the Totonacs (an indigenous people of what is now Mexico), then embraced by Aztecs, who conquered the Totonacs and used vanilla to flavor a chocolate beverage. In the early 1500s, when Hernán Cortés and his fellow conquistadors forcefully conquered the Aztec, they took vanilla (along with silver and chocolate) back home.

What the Spaniards stole was a cutting from a single vanilla orchid, which was propagated throughout the Western colonial empire. In fact, this lone cutting is the great-great-great (et cetera!) grandmother of the majority of the world's vanilla, according to Alan Chambers, a professor at the University of Florida focused on the genetics of tropical fruit and one of my vanilla gurus.

The clones of that cutting, rooted in water during its transatlantic voyage and ultimately planted, grew well in equatorial climates and, in particular, on French-controlled Réunion, an island in the Indian Ocean just east of Madagascar. There was just one issue—the orchid bore no fruit. The missing ingredient, it turns out, was the plant's main pollinator, the itty-bitty Melipona bee, which was nonexistent outside Central America. And so, for three centuries, even though the plant thrived, the secrets of the plant remained a mystery.

It was on Réunion that young Edmond Albius, an enslaved worker, figured out how to pollinate the pods, replicating the bees' activity using a narrow stick, and vanilla bean production exploded. Still, it's painstaking work. The stick must lift the tiny, delicate membrane that separates the male and female parts of the plant, and then the farmer must gently press those parts together. To produce the seedpods, *every* last flower on the long, climbing vines must be pollinated by hand. Add to that, the vanilla orchid plays hard to get. The flowers bloom for a single day each year and they're only fertile for up to twelve hours after blooming. Miss that window or injure the blossoms, and you risk precious pods. And *on top of that*, farmers find themselves with the precarious task of balancing how many flowers to pollinate to ensure maximum revenue and how many to prune to ensure the plant has enough life force for each bean to ripen properly and fetch top dollar at the market.

Nine months postpollination, babies are born in the form of lots of green seedpods, which will ripen, then be harvested and sold, though the process is far from over. Now, curing begins. The specifics vary, but often the pods are plunged into hot water, which coaxes out the enzymes that begin to transform the odorless pod into fragrant vanilla beans. Still hot from the water, the blanched beans are then meticulously sweated—wrapped in wool blankets and enclosed in airtight containers—and over the course of two months, artisans balance keeping them warm and preventing mold by wrapping and unwrapping, moving them into the sun and hiding them from rain (including during monsoon season). For another month, the beans are dried, and workers must toggle sun and shade and massage the beans daily to achieve even drying and precise moisture content. Finally, they're enclosed in a box for yet another month, and only then do you have the dark, glossy, wrinkly, wildly fragrant triumph that is . . . "boring" old vanilla.

BUYING VANILLA

Real vanilla is a victim of its own glory. Spikes in the price for vanilla beans lead to huge surges of money around harvest time, as big exporters fund middlemen with cash advances to buy green seedpods to be sweated and dried. The closer farmers get to a well-deserved payday, the more they're in danger. To head off thieves, many farmers choose to harvest early, when the pods aren't quite ripe, often hiding the beans under mattresses until the government-approved "harvest period." And ultimately quality suffers. So, as it often does, the safety and prosperity of farmers go hand in hand with quality.

That's why we buy vanilla from a company that considers the needs of farmers. Singing Dog, based in Eugene, Oregon, gives small farmers in Indonesia and Papua New Guinea a stake in their vanilla, paying both market price and offering a percentage of sales. That way everyone's interests dovetail—high-quality beans mean more money for all. And the beans are truly top-notch.

Now, I love using whole vanilla pods. But sometimes, if a pastry chef tells me, with swagger, that they only use whole pods, I will politely explain why I prefer vanilla extract. The way I see it, the dried pod is somewhere between fruit and tea—its flavor has developed and intensified through the drying and curing process and needs to be unlocked. Steeping split pods in neutral alcohol slowly and efficiently extracts all those compounds. Not to mention that extract is more readily available, lasts far longer in your pantry, and costs less, ounce for ounce, than whole beans.

For most of our ice creams, we use Singing Dog's double-fold extract (aka double-strength). While most "pure" extracts are single-fold (13.35 ounces of vanilla bean per gallon of 70-proof alcohol), double-fold packs in 26.7 ounces, and you can really taste the difference. Singing Dog's double-fold was formerly only available to commercial operations, but when the first Salt & Straw cookbook mentioned how incredible it is, people came calling, and the demand was so great that Singing Dog made it available for retail purchase. And while our options were previously limited, today we can choose several varieties of bean and extracts with different flavor profiles. Here are the big three:

- **Mexican Vanilla:** Subject to drastic hybridization by native local vanilla strains, it reminds me, in a good way, of Cherry Coke.
- **Bourbon (aka Madagascar) Vanilla:** Named not for the brown spirit but for the island of Réunion, formerly called Île Bourbon. It has lovely Cuban cigar vibes.
- **Tahitian Vanilla:** Not necessarily grown in Tahiti but on any number of the hundred-plus islands that make up French Polynesia, of which Tahiti is the best known. It brings to mind, with its notes of tropical fruit and spiced rum, a piña colada.

THE SPECS ON SPECKS

At home, working with vanilla beans allows you to get those classic black specks from the seeds inside the pods. If you ask me, a scoop of plain vanilla isn't quite whole without them. At Salt & Straw, however, we buy our specks. After artisans make extracts, the spent pods are dried, ground, and sold with the specific purpose of providing ice cream makers like us with some aesthetic discretion—it's a kind of food coloring, if you will. At home, "vanilla bean paste" (a mixture of extract, ground pods, and cornstarch) serves a similar purpose.

Grade A
Vanilla
tahitensis

Grade B
Vanilla
tahitensis

Grade A
Vanilla
planifolia

Grade B
Vanilla
planifolia

Extract
Grade
Vanilla
planifolia

Rejected/
Ungraded
Vanilla
planifolia

BOURBON BROWN SUGAR VANILLA

Vanilla, bourbon, and brown sugar are an amazing flavor trinity that completely transforms basic cocktails (try brown sugar and vanilla bitters in your next old-fashioned), cakes, cookies, and especially ice cream. The bourbon's oaky, butterscotch-y undertones and the slightly astringent molasses notes in brown sugar echo those in good vanilla, heightening its pleasures.

MAKES ABOUT
1½ PINTS

¼ cup lightly packed light brown sugar

2 tablespoons bourbon

2 teaspoons pure vanilla extract

3 cups 17% Butterfat Base (page 22)

In a medium bowl, stir together the brown sugar, bourbon, and vanilla. It's okay if the sugar isn't fully dissolved. Stir in the ice cream base.

Pour the mixture into an ice cream maker and turn on the machine. Churn just until it has the texture of soft serve, 30 to 40 minutes, depending on the machine.

Transfer to freezer-safe containers and freeze until firm, at least 6 hours. It keeps for up to 3 months. (See Freezing & Storage, page 15, for tips.)

VANILLA
WITH CARAMELIZED WHITE CHOCOLATE

White chocolate tastes like vanilla. After all, there aren't any cocoa solids in it. To add flavor, the best makers add real vanilla extract. (If you're not a fan of white chocolate, I'd bet you've tried only the stuff made with one-dimensional vanillin. Check those ingredient lists, friends!) I lean into that complex vanilla flavor here, plus I toast the chips, which caramelizes them so they taste beguilingly complex.

MAKES ABOUT
2 PINTS

½ cup white chocolate chips

3 cups 17% Butterfat Base (page 22)

2 teaspoons pure vanilla extract

2 teaspoons Diamond Crystal kosher salt

Preheat the oven to 350°F.

Spread the white chocolate on a small baking sheet and bake until the chocolate turns an even amber color, 3 to 4 minutes.

Scrape the warm chocolate into a medium bowl, add the ice cream base, vanilla, and salt and use a stick blender (or transfer to a stand blender) to blend until smooth.

Pour the mixture into an ice cream maker and turn on the machine. Churn just until it has the texture of soft serve, 30 to 40 minutes, depending on the machine.

Transfer to freezer-safe containers and freeze until firm, at least 6 hours or for up to 3 months. (See Freezing & Storage, page 15, for tips.)

HONEY-ROASTED BANANA VANILLA

MAKES ABOUT
2 PINTS

Standard banana ice cream tastes kind of like bananas. But I wanted mine to *really* taste like bananas. So I borrowed a trick I learned from Kir Jensen, one of Portland's coolest pastry chefs, and slathered the fruit with honey and then roasted it in the oven to concentrate the flavor. This worked wonders, yet it's our good friend vanilla that takes the scoop from intensely banana-y (good) to omg-am-I-eating-frozen-banana-pudding (great). For an extra boost of banana flavor, rewrap the honey-slathered banana in its peel before sticking it in the oven.

1	ripe banana
1	tablespoon honey
⅛	teaspoon ground nutmeg
3	cups 17% Butterfat Base (page 22)
2	teaspoons pure vanilla extract
1	teaspoon Diamond Crystal kosher salt

Preheat the oven to 350°F. Line a small baking sheet with parchment paper.

Peel the banana, reserving the peel. Rub the banana with the honey, sprinkle with the nutmeg, then drape the peel back over the banana. Bake on the lined baking sheet until the peel turns dark brown and the flesh is super tender, about 10 minutes.

Discard the peel. In a medium bowl, mash the banana until smooth, add the ice cream base, vanilla, and salt and stir until smooth.

Pour the mixture into an ice cream maker and turn on the machine. Churn just until it has the texture of soft serve, 30 to 40 minutes, depending on the machine.

Transfer to freezer-safe containers and freeze until firm, at least 6 hours or for up to 3 months. (See Freezing & Storage, page 15, for tips.)

SMOKED-CHERRY VANILLA

MAKES ABOUT
2 PINTS

2   tablespoons lapsang
    souchong tea leaves

½   cup preserved Amarena
    cherries (or Luxardo
    brand maraschino
    cherries), plus
    2 tablespoons of
    their syrup

3   cups 17% Butterfat
    Base (page 22)

2   teaspoons pure
    vanilla extract

I first started smoking vanilla twelve years ago to add a campfire-evoking element to a Foie Gras S'mores flavor, a collaboration with my friends Greg and Gaby Denton of Ox Restaurant here in Portland. We settled on hot-boxing vanilla beans with smoldering cherrywood chips, then steeping the beans in alcohol for thirty days to make a smoked vanilla extract. That heady creation spawned this less-demanding play on cherry vanilla, which looks to preserved Amarena cherries for their wallop of stone-fruit flavor and lapsang souchong tea for a smoky, almost savory dimension.

Microwave ¼ cup water in a mug until steaming, about 30 seconds. Add the lapsang souchong leaves and steep the tea for 6 minutes. Strain and let cool, discarding the leaves.

Chop the cherries into pebble-sized pieces.

In the bowl of the ice cream maker, combine the tea, cherries, cherry syrup, ice cream base, and vanilla and turn on the machine. Churn just until it has the texture of soft serve, 30 to 40 minutes, depending on the machine.

Transfer to freezer-safe containers and freeze until firm, at least 6 hours or for up to 3 months. (See Freezing & Storage, page 15, for tips.)

VANILLA CUSTARD
WITH BUTTERSCOTCH SWIRLS

MAKES ABOUT
2½ PINTS

3   cups Rich Custard Base
    (page 24)

1   teaspoon pure vanilla
    extract

⅛   teaspoon Diamond Crystal
    kosher salt

½   cup Butterscotch Swirl
    (opposite)

Butterscotch is one of my favorite ways to play up the romantic smoky flavors of good vanilla. It doesn't hurt that the confection is even easier to make than its cousin, caramel, because it doesn't rely on the finicky burning of sugar for its beautiful bitter edge. Instead, it leans into the bittersweet character inherent in brown sugar (its color comes from molasses). The reason for the "scotch" part of the name seems lost to history—apparently, the classic contained no whisky whatsoever. But oddly enough, this recipe tastes *way* better *with* Scotch (my pick is the super-peaty, briny Laphroaig). It makes me wonder if the misnomer wasn't actually a happy linguistic accident that foretold the secret to making even better butterscotch.

In a medium bowl, combine the ice cream base, vanilla, and salt and whisk to combine.

Pour the mixture into an ice cream maker and turn on the machine. Churn just until it has the texture of soft serve, 30 to 40 minutes, depending on the machine.

Quickly alternate spooning layers of the ice cream and swirls of butterscotch into freezer-safe containers.

Freeze until firm, at least 6 hours or for up to 3 months. (See Freezing & Storage, page 15, for tips.)

BUTTERSCOTCH SWIRL

MAKES ABOUT 1 CUP

⅔ cup heavy cream

2 tablespoons peaty, slightly smoky Scotch (I love Laphroaig here)

1 teaspoon Diamond Crystal kosher salt

¾ cup light brown sugar

¼ cup light corn syrup

4 tablespoons (½ stick) unsalted butter

1 tablespoon cornstarch

In a small bowl, stir together the heavy cream, Scotch, and salt and set aside.

In a small saucepan, combine the brown sugar, corn syrup, and butter. Cook over medium-high heat, stirring often, until the mixture just starts to smoke, about 5 minutes. Turn off the heat, then immediately add the heavy cream mixture and whisk until completely combined. If there are any clumps of hardened sugar, cook over low heat, whisking constantly, until they melt.

In a cup, stir together the cornstarch and 1 tablespoon water with a fork until smooth. Pour the cornstarch slurry into the saucepan and whisk until combined. Cook over medium-low heat, whisking frequently, until the butterscotch has thickened slightly, about 3 minutes.

Let the butterscotch cool to where it can still be drizzled but is not so warm that it would melt the ice cream base. If not using immediately, let it cool to room temperature, transfer to an airtight container, and refrigerate for up to 2 weeks. Separation is normal. Just stir well before using and either let it warm up on the counter or place in a small saucepan to warm slightly over low heat.

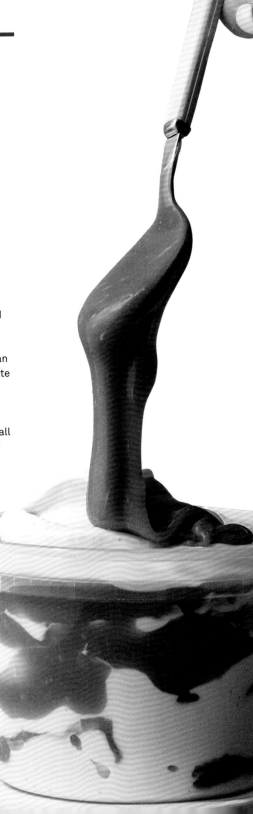

BIRTHDAY CAKE & BLACKBERRIES

MAKES ABOUT
2 PINTS

3   cups 17% Butterfat Base
    (page 22)

1   teaspoon pure vanilla
    extract

¼   teaspoon clear
    (imitation) vanilla
    extract

1   teaspoon Diamond Crystal
    kosher salt

½   cup Birthday Cake
    Crumble (recipe follows)

½   cup blackberry jam,
    stirred to loosen

Vanilla and birthday cake go together like milk and cookies—and not just any vanilla: that clear artificial stuff that defines boxed cake mix and tugs at my heartstrings. Here, birthday cake shows up in the form of rainbow sprinkle-strewn shortbread-esque cookies flavored with both real and ersatz vanilla. It's what pastry chefs—such as, famously, the great Christina Tosi of Milk Bar—often refer to as a crumble, crunch, or gravel. It's full of enough fat to resist sogging out, so each spoonful has crunchy, crumbly explosions of "Happy Birthday!" fun.

In the early days of Salt & Straw, I'd bake an entire sheet tray of the heavenly birthday cake crumble and eat it by the handful, along with fresh blackberries, but in the scoop, we use blackberry jam, which stays gooey when frozen. The whole thing is *almost* too sweet, just like the best birthday cake always is.

In a medium bowl, combine the ice cream base, both vanillas, and the salt and whisk until smooth.

Pour the mixture into an ice cream maker and turn on the machine. Churn just until the mixture has the texture of soft serve, 30 to 40 minutes, depending on the machine.

Use a spoon or flexible spatula to gently fold the birthday cake crumbles into the ice cream so they're well distributed. Quickly alternate spooning layers of the mixture into freezer-safe containers and dolloping about 1 tablespoon of the jam over each spoonful.

Freeze until firm, at least 6 hours or for up to 3 months. (See Freezing & Storage, page 15, for tips.)

• recipe continues •

BIRTHDAY CAKE CRUMBLE

MAKES ABOUT 2 CUPS

½ cup all-purpose flour

⅓ cup granulated sugar

4 tablespoons (½ stick) unsalted butter, melted

2 tablespoons rainbow sprinkles

1 tablespoon pure vanilla extract

1 tablespoon light brown sugar

½ teaspoon baking powder

½ teaspoon Diamond Crystal kosher salt

Preheat the oven to 325°F. Line a sheet pan with parchment paper.

In a stand mixer fitted with the paddle, combine the flour, granulated sugar, melted butter, sprinkles, vanilla, brown sugar, baking powder, and salt and mix on medium speed until the butter is fully incorporated, about 2 minutes.

Use your hands to sprinkle the crumble onto the sheet pan in an even layer, breaking up any lingering large chunks into pea-size pieces.

Bake until the crumble is evenly crisped and light golden brown, about 12 minutes, rotating the sheet pan front to back halfway through. Let it cool to room temperature.

Break up any large chunks that may have fused while baking and store in an airtight container in the freezer until ready to use or for up to 2 months.

PASSION FRUIT VANILLA
WITH EXTRA-DARK CHOCOLATE FUDGE

**MAKES ABOUT
2 PINTS**

1 tablespoon granulated sugar

⅓ cup chopped (chip-size pieces) good dark chocolate

2 tablespoons frozen passion fruit puree, thawed

3 cups Vegan Coconut Base (page 27)

1 teaspoon pure vanilla extract

⅛ teaspoon Diamond Crystal kosher salt

1 vanilla bean, split lengthwise

1 cup Extra-Dark Chocolate Fudge Sauce (recipe follows)

In the wine world, they say "What grows together, goes together," and it's true. But as my friend Sebastian Cisneros, from Portland's Cloudforest chocolate factory, showed me, the principle doesn't just apply to pairing Barolo with truffles. He grew up in Ecuador and has relationships with farmers who grow vanilla, chocolate, and passion fruit, and guess what? Together, they taste fantastic, particularly with a bright, fruity chocolate that echoes the tart, tropical wallop of the passion fruit. The flavor of vanilla is restrained here, but it's also the reason the combination works.

In a small saucepan, combine ¼ cup water and the sugar and cook over medium heat, stirring occasionally, until the sugar has completely dissolved, about 3 minutes. Turn off the heat, add the chocolate chips, and stir with a flexible spatula until the chocolate has melted completely, about 2 minutes. Let the chocolate syrup cool to room temp.

In a medium bowl, combine the chocolate syrup, 1 tablespoon of the passion fruit puree, and 1½ cups of the coconut base.

In a second medium bowl, combine the remaining 1 tablespoon passion fruit puree, the vanilla extract, salt, and the remaining 1½ cups coconut base. Scrape in the vanilla seeds. Cover and stick the bowl in the fridge while you churn the chocolate ice cream. (Depending on your ice cream maker, you may need to refrigerate overnight; see Note, page 49.)

Pour the chocolate-coconut mixture into an ice cream maker and turn on the machine. Churn just until the mixture has the texture of soft serve, 15 to 20 minutes, depending on the machine.

Quickly transfer the chocolate ice cream to freezer-safe containers, filling each container only about halfway. Drizzle the fudge all along the surface, cover, and store the containers in the freezer while you churn the vanilla ice cream (see Note, page 49).

Pour the vanilla-coconut mixture into an ice cream maker and turn on the machine. Churn just until the mixture has the texture of soft serve, 15 to 20 minutes, depending on the machine.

Quickly transfer the vanilla ice cream into the containers of chocolate ice cream, filling all of the nooks and crannies of each container.

Freeze until firm, at least 6 hours or for up to 3 months. (See Freezing & Storage, page 15, for tips.)

• recipe continues •

AMERICA'S MOST ICONIC ICE CREAMS

EXTRA-DARK CHOCOLATE FUDGE SAUCE

MAKES ABOUT 2 CUPS

½ cup granulated sugar

½ cup light corn syrup

⅔ cup coconut cream

1 tablespoon unsalted butter

2 teaspoons black cocoa powder or any unsweetened cocoa powder

⅛ teaspoon xanthan gum

½ teaspoon Diamond Crystal kosher salt

¾ cup chopped (chip-size pieces) good dark chocolate

In a small saucepan, combine the sugar, corn syrup, coconut cream, and butter and heat over medium-low heat, whisking constantly, until the mixture comes to a simmer. Add the cocoa powder, xanthan gum, and salt and continue to whisk until the mixture looks smooth (no clumps!) and glossy, about 1 minute.

Remove from the heat and add the chocolate. Whisk until the chocolate pieces are completely melted and the fudge is smooth. Let cool to room temperature before using.

The fudge keeps in an airtight container in the fridge for up to 2 weeks. Bring to room temperature and stir well before using.

VANILLA
WITH STICKY CROISSANTS AND CARAMEL SWIRLS

MAKES ABOUT
2 PINTS

3   cups Rich Custard
    Base (page 24)

1   tablespoon plus
    ½ teaspoon pure
    vanilla extract

¾   cup Cinnamon-Spiced
    Caramel (opposite)

1   cup Twice-Baked Honey
    Croissants (opposite)

If only I could take credit for creating this flavor. But that honor goes to Autumn, a Portland fourth grader, who submitted to our Student Inventor program the idea of incorporating croissants into ice cream. Her goal was to make you "feel like you are in France," so we chose to make a decadent frozen custard with a silky texture reminiscent of crème brûlée and pastry cream, and then we fold in croissants that have been flattened and honey-coated to accentuate and preserve the flaky shatter in each scoop.

In a medium bowl, whisk together the ice cream base and vanilla.

Pour the mixture into an ice cream maker and turn on the machine. Churn just until it has the texture of soft serve, 30 to 40 minutes, depending on the machine.

Meanwhile, put the caramel in a warm place or warm it in a small saucepan over very low heat just until it's drizzle-able, but not so warm that it'll melt the ice cream.

Use a spoon or flexible spatula to gently fold the croissant pieces into the ice cream so they're well distributed. Quickly alternate spooning layers of the ice cream and drizzling on a generous spiral of caramel into freezer-safe containers.

Freeze until firm, at least 6 hours or for up to 3 months. (See Freezing & Storage, page 15, for tips.)

CINNAMON-SPICED CARAMEL

MAKES ABOUT 2 CUPS

1½ cups granulated sugar

¼ cup light corn syrup

1¼ cups heavy cream

2 tablespoons unsalted butter, cut into several pieces

½ teaspoon Diamond Crystal kosher salt

1 teaspoon ground cinnamon

In a medium pot, stir together the sugar, corn syrup, and ¼ cup water until all of the sugar looks wet. Cover, set the pan over medium-high heat, and cook, stirring occasionally, until the sugar has completely melted, about 3 minutes.

Continue to cook, covered, but this time *without* stirring, until the mixture has thickened slightly, about 3 minutes.

Uncover and continue cooking, without stirring but paying close attention, until the mixture turns the color of light maple syrup, about 3 minutes more.

Take the pan off the heat, and right away (with your face a safe distance from the pan!) begin gradually pouring in the cream, stirring as you pour. Pour slowly at

first and then speed up to a nice steady stream. (Whatever you do, do not dump in the cream all at once!)

Put the pan over medium-high heat again. Attach a candy thermometer to the side of the pan. Let the mixture simmer away, stirring occasionally, until it registers about 230°F on the thermometer, about 3 minutes. Take the pan off the heat and whisk in the butter, salt, and cinnamon until the butter has completely melted and there are no clumps of cinnamon.

Let the caramel cool to room temperature, then use it right away or transfer it to an airtight container and refrigerate it for up to 2 weeks. Separation is totally normal; just make sure to stir the caramel well before using it.

TWICE-BAKED HONEY CROISSANTS

MAKES ABOUT 4 CUPS OF CROISSANT PIECES

2 croissants (the yummier the better)

¼ cup honey

¼ cup granulated sugar

¼ teaspoon Diamond Crystal kosher salt

Preheat the oven to 350°F. Line a baking sheet with parchment paper.

Press the croissants with the palm of your hand to flatten them to about ¼ inch thick. Cut the smashed croissants into roughly ½-inch pieces. Leaving behind any crumbs, transfer the croissants to the baking sheet. Drizzle the honey on top of the croissants and toss together until evenly coated. Sprinkle the sugar and salt on top of the croissants, toss again until evenly coated, and spread in a single layer.

Bake until the croissants are toasty and crisp at the edges, about 15 minutes.

Let the croissants cool to room temperature. Store them in an airtight container in the freezer until you're ready to use them as a mix-in (or to simply eat them) or for up to 3 months. There's no need to thaw the pieces before using them in the ice cream.

NOTE · YOU'LL HAVE SOME OF THE LOVELY PEACHY, WINEY COOKING LIQUID LEFT OVER— AND YOU'RE GOING TO TURN IT INTO A KILLER ICE CREAM (OR YOGURT) TOPPER. JUST TURN UP THE HEAT AND SIMMER UNTIL IT REDUCES TO A THICK SYRUP. LET IT COOL AND GET DRIZZLING.

VANILLA POACHED PEACH GELATO

MAKES ABOUT
2½ PINTS

Peaches are glorious in ice cream, not that you'd know it from the typical peach ice cream. You see, peaches, like strawberries, have a delicate flavor, and without a little strategic manipulation, that lovely peachiness just gets obscured by the fat necessary to make a properly creamy scoop. The trick here is twofold: (1) Scale back, just a little, on the fat, which is why we choose gelato over ice cream, and (2) buy ripe, high-season peaches and intensify their essence by perking up the acid with white wine and hitting them hard with vanilla to bolster their natural flavor.

POACHED PEACHES

1   cup white wine
    (I prefer a sweeter
    wine like Pinot Blanc
    or Riesling)

2   tablespoons honey

2   vanilla beans,
    preferably Tahitian,
    split lengthwise

2   very ripe yellow
    peaches, peeled,
    halved, and pitted

ICE CREAM

3   cups Gelato Base
    (page 25)

    Finely grated zest
    and juice of 1 lemon

¼   teaspoon Diamond
    Crystal kosher salt

¾   cup peach jam, well
    stirred to loosen

POACH THE PEACHES

In a medium saucepan, combine the wine and honey. Scrape the vanilla bean seeds into the pot, add the pods, and bring it to a simmer over medium heat. Reduce the heat to maintain a lazy simmer, add the peaches, cover the pan, and cook, flipping the peaches halfway through, until completely tender but not falling apart, about 15 minutes.

Reserving the poaching liquid and discarding the vanilla pod, transfer the peaches to a blender and let them cool until they're warm to the touch.

Add 2 tablespoons of the poaching liquid and blend to a smooth puree. (What to do with the rest of the poaching liquid? See Note!) For an even silkier mixture, pour the puree through a fine-mesh sieve, stirring and pressing with a spoon, to remove any remaining fibers.

CHURN THE ICE CREAM

In a medium bowl, combine the gelato base, lemon zest, lemon juice, salt, and 1 cup of the peach puree and whisk until smooth. (Stir any remaining peach puree into the syrup; see Note.)

Pour the mixture into an ice cream maker and turn on the machine. Churn just until it has the texture of soft serve, 30 to 40 minutes, depending on the machine.

Quickly alternate spooning layers of the ice cream into freezer-safe containers and dolloping about 1 tablespoon of the jam over each spoonful. Freeze until firm, at least 6 hours or for up to 3 months. (See Freezing & Storage, page 15, for tips.)

Choc

Hershey's-ification be damned, the cacao bean is an incredible artisanal product that through careful farming, fermenting, drying, and roasting blossoms into a product with peerless flavor and endless nuance. Here we explore its many facets in frozen form.

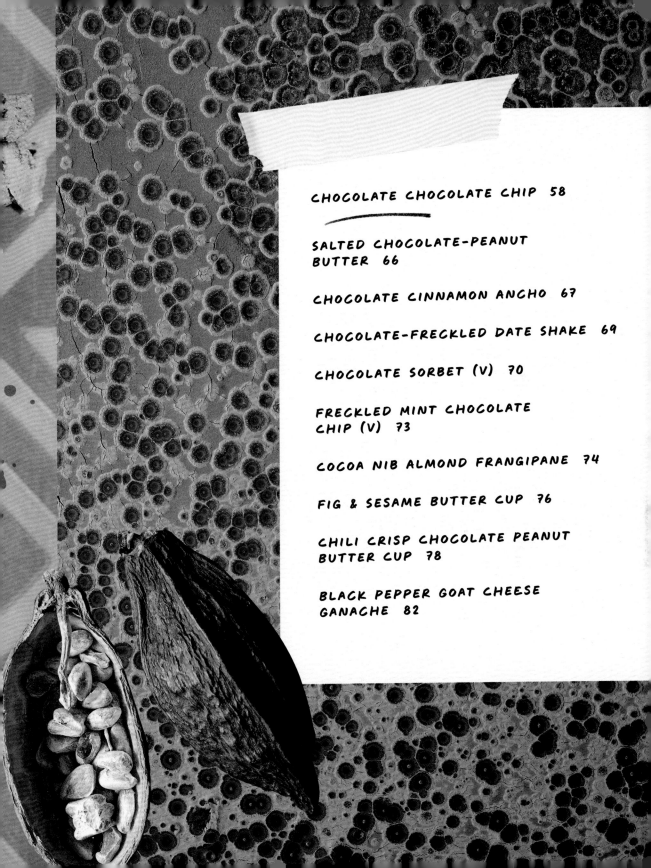

CHOCOLATE CHOCOLATE CHIP 58

SALTED CHOCOLATE-PEANUT
BUTTER 66

CHOCOLATE CINNAMON ANCHO 67

CHOCOLATE-FRECKLED DATE SHAKE 69

CHOCOLATE SORBET (V) 70

FRECKLED MINT CHOCOLATE
CHIP (V) 73

COCOA NIB ALMOND FRANGIPANE 74

FIG & SESAME BUTTER CUP 76

CHILI CRISP CHOCOLATE PEANUT
BUTTER CUP 78

BLACK PEPPER GOAT CHEESE
GANACHE 82

OUR ULTIMATE

CHOCOLATE CHOCOLATE CHIP

**MAKES ABOUT
2 PINTS**

3   cups 17% Butterfat
     Base (page 22)

½   cup Chocolate Mom
     (opposite)

¾   cup chopped (chip-
     size pieces) good
     dark chocolate

2   teaspoons vegetable
     oil

Chocolate ice cream could be more accurately described as cocoa powder ice cream. Less sexy, I know, since the word "chocolate" brings to mind a prettily wrapped bar, the snap of chocolate that melts in your mouth, enrobing your taste buds.

Thing is, you sorta have to use cocoa powder to flavor your ice cream. You see, cocoa butter just doesn't freeze like butterfat, and cocoa powder (essentially just the cocoa solids) has only trace amounts. Which is all well and good, except most cocoa powder is just not that delicious. And there's a reason: The vast majority of cocoa is a by-product of the far more valuable cocoa butter, which is produced not to be eaten so much as applied to your face and hands as lotion and makeup. The farmers supplying these cacao beans aren't growing them for flavor but to max out on that precious cocoa butter.

So to make our version of the classic, we hunt down the good stuff, a cocoa powder with intense aroma and complex flavor. Meridian Cacao, Valrhona, and Guittard Cocoa Rouge are three great options. (More generally, look for cocoa powder with higher fat content—it'll be right there on the nutrition facts— which suggests the maker's priority wasn't wringing out cocoa butter for making hand lotion.) We heat the powder with water and sugar until it's nice and glossy—we call it Chocolate Mom, because like our moms, it gives us so much.

Second, we ensure the ice cream delivers some of the pleasure of the chocolate bar experience. Mixing in bits of chocolate, the typical move, doesn't work, as anyone knows who's ever encountered those waxy bits that taste of chocolate only after they finally melt. That's because chocolate is tempered—a process of stabilizing the chocolate (more on that later)—so it melts at around 90°F (that is, in your mouth, not in your hand). That's great when chocolate is in bar form but not so great when you're serving it at 10°F in a scoop and it takes a loooong time to warm up enough to enjoy. Instead, we effectively re-temper the chocolate: We melt it, mix in a touch of oil, and stir it into fresh churned ice cream, which creates thin shards of chocolate (this is known as stracciatella, Italian for "little rags"). The shards melt at 70°F instead of 90°F. And that 20°F difference is huge. After you experience the delicate snap of biting through the shards, the chocolate quickly liquefies for a wallop of flavor.

In the bowl of an ice cream maker, combine the ice cream base and Chocolate Mom and turn on the machine. Churn just until it has the texture of soft serve, 30 to 40 minutes, depending on the machine.

While the ice cream is churning, pour an inch or so of water into a small saucepan and bring it to a simmer. In a heatproof bowl that can sit in the saucepan without touching the water, combine the chocolate and vegetable oil. Set the bowl over the saucepan, reduce the heat to low, and heat, stirring occasionally, until the chocolate is completely melted, about 2 minutes. Take the pan off the heat, but leave the bowl on the pan. The chocolate will stay warm until the ice cream is churned.

Once the ice cream is ready, quickly alternate spooning layers of the ice cream and drizzling on a generous spiral of melted chocolate into freezer-safe containers.

Freeze until firm, at least 6 hours or for up to 3 months. (See Freezing & Storage, page 15, for tips.)

CHOCOLATE MOM

MAKES ABOUT ½ CUP

⅓ cup cocoa powder

¼ cup granulated sugar

In a small saucepan, whisk together the cocoa powder, sugar, and ¼ cup water. Set over medium heat and cook, stirring slowly and constantly, until the cocoa powder is no longer in clumps and the mixture looks glossy, about 3 minutes. Let cool to room temperature.

Store in an airtight container in the fridge for up to 2 weeks. Microwave for about 30 seconds and stir in order to loosen before using in ice cream.

NOTE · OVERACHIEVERS, I'M NOT SAYING YOU HAVE TO, BUT YOU COULD MAKE YOURSELF THREE SEPARATE BATCHES OF CHOCOLATE MOM—ONE WITH DUTCH-PROCESS COCOA, ONE WITH NATURAL, AND ANOTHER WITH EXTRA-ALKALIZED COCOA ROUGE—AND THEN TINKER LIKE A MAD SCIENTIST TO FORMULATE A FLAVOR PROFILE THAT REALLY SINGS TO YOUR TASTE BUDS. JUST BE SURE TO COOK THE SYRUPS UNTIL THE COCOA POWDER LOSES ITS STARCHY TEXTURE—A GORGEOUS GLOSSY LOOK IS A TELLTALE SIGN, BUT THERE'S NO SHAME IN THE DIP-AND-LICK METHOD OF TESTING.

FOOD OF THE GODS

Before I fell down my first chocolate rabbit hole years ago, I assumed that much of chocolate's appeal could be traced to the heaps of sugar it's typically paired with. Au contraire. Keep in mind that when the Olmecs (and later the Mayans and then the Aztecs) so revered cacao—thousands of years before Europeans had set eyes upon the fruit—they drank it as a bitter, chile-spiked beverage, taken hot or cold. Only occasionally was it sweetened with a little honey. The Aztecs, after all, named it *xocolatl*—Nahuatl for "bitter water." Even without sugar, chocolate was special enough that these cacao trailblazers considered it a gift from the gods.

When the Spanish conquistadors arrived in Mesoamerica in the early sixteenth century and subsequently brought the first cacao to Europe, it took almost no time (in the grand scheme of history, at least) for its use to explode. Soon the Spanish were importing cacao to Europe—where drinking sweet chocolate was all the rage—as well as shipping it to the American colonies. There was just something magical about chocolate. In 1841, shortly before the chocolate bar was invented, a Russian chemist identified cacao's principal alkaloid, the compound that might be responsible for chocolate's profound appeal. He named it theobromine after *Theobroma cacao*, the scientific name for the tree it came from, which itself means "food of the gods."

This discovery was a possible answer to a question so many of us have had: Why do we love chocolate so much? Research into theobromine suggests that this affection may have a biochemical basis. Theobromine has a composition very similar to caffeine, another compound in cacao—in fact, caffeine is broken down by the body into theobromine—but its effect is a little different. While caffeine's effect can tip into jitters and dependence (and unpleasant withdrawal symptoms), theobromine has a gentler stimulant effect that may mellow out that of caffeine. The synergy produces pleasure.

That said, ascribing specific effects to components in isolation is a tricky business. So while it's true that fine dark chocolate both has more theobromine than chocolate-flavored confections that are mostly milk and sugar *and* makes us feel more elated, it's also true that dark chocolate has the benefit of being incredibly delicious. Deliciousness has its own gastrophysics—the dopamine rush of a tasty treat is no joke.

Credit for the existence of the cacao tree might belong to God (or nature), but it's people who figured out how to turn this oblong fruit into something divine.

BUYING CHOCOLATE

To consider the fruit of the cacao tree is to be in awe of the fact that the glorious creation of chocolate exists at all. That Mesoamerican civilizations managed to turn the pulpy seeds of this fruit into a foodstuff more valuable than gold is a miracle of vision and culinary chemistry. Nowadays, the fruit yields many delicious products, all with wondrous applications in our ice cream recipes. Here's what you need to know.

COCOA NIBS: Before there is chocolate, there are nibs. After the cacao seeds are removed from the fruit pods, they're fermented, dried, roasted, and cracked. Remove the shells and you're left with so-called nibs, a pure form of chocolate that has a complex, earthy flavor and pleasant astringency.

COCOA POWDER: Cacao seeds are composed of cocoa solids and cocoa butter. When ground up, they produce something called chocolate liquor. This is what is used to make solid chocolates—bars, chips, and the like. But for cocoa powder, the nibs are pressed to extract the cocoa butter (for use in chocolate making as well as in skincare and beauty products), leaving behind the cocoa solids—and inevitably a little fat. This residue is pulverized to make cocoa powder, often known as natural-process cocoa powder to distinguish it from Dutch-process cocoa powder. Natural-process cocoa has an intense, bitter, slightly fruity flavor. Dutch-process cocoa, so-named because a Dutch chocolate maker came up with the idea, is cocoa powder that's been alkalized to lower its acidity. It's darker in color and less bitter. There are also different levels of alkalization that produce different kinds of Dutch-process cocoa powder, including black cocoa powder, most famous for its presence in Oreos.

CHOCOLATE: After nibs are ground into chocolate liquor, then they're "conched," or treated to another grinding process along with sugar, additional cocoa butter, and milk (for milk chocolate), which produces that creamy, velvety texture we love. Finally, the chocolate is tempered—carefully and precisely heated to change the structure of its fat—so that it looks glossy, snaps gloriously when you bite it, and melts on your tongue and not in your hands.

Strangely, terms like dark, bittersweet, or semisweet chocolate are unregulated. Let the cocoa percentages be your guide. These refer to the ratio of chocolate to sugar. Chocolate labeled 70% cocoa (or cacao), for instance, has 30% sugar and the rest is cocoa (fat and solids). In general, the lower the cocoa percentage, the sweeter and less chocolatey the taste. White chocolate contains no cocoa solids but lots of cocoa butter. Despite what some claim, it's very much real chocolate, just without the bitterness of those solids.

CHOCOLATE CHIPS: This is tempered chocolate made into cute little chips. Because the best chocolate is often sold in bar form, I recommend buying a nice bar and chopping it into roughly chip-size pieces for the recipes in this book.

COCOA POWDER GUIDE

Meridian Single-Origin Natural Cocoa

Guittard Cocoa Rouge

Cacao Barry Black Cocoa

TCHO High-Fat Natural Cocoa

Valrhona Dutch-Processed Cocoa

SALTED CHOCOLATE– PEANUT BUTTER

MAKES ABOUT 2 PINTS

3 cups 17% Butterfat Base (page 22)

½ cup Chocolate Mom (page 59)

1 teaspoon Diamond Crystal kosher salt

1 cup creamy peanut butter (I love Skippy Natural)

⅓ cup confectioners' sugar

It won't come as news that peanut butter and chocolate are a heavenly match, but the revelation here is what peanut butter does for chocolate ice cream. Not only does PB's nutty flavor heighten the chocolate's and its natural fat make the finished scoop extra creamy, it also allows for this cool trick: After churning, we fold in peanut butter that freezes into decadent shards not unlike those in stracciatella.

This peanut-butter marbling can be applied to so many ice creams. It's especially good, for instance, in Roasted Strawberries with Japanese Whiskey (page 99)—hello, fancy PB&J!—and Salted Pretzel Ice Cream (page 134), because, obvs. Mixing confectioners' sugar into the peanut butter helps those shards melt more quickly on your tongue.

In a medium bowl, stir together the ice cream base, Chocolate Mom, salt, and ½ cup of the peanut butter.

Pour the mixture into an ice cream maker and turn on the machine. Churn just until it has the texture of soft serve, 30 to 40 minutes, depending on the machine.

While the ice cream churns, in a small bowl, combine the confectioners' sugar and remaining ½ cup peanut butter and stir until fully combined.

When the ice cream has finished churning, use a spoon or flexible spatula to gently fold the sweetened peanut butter mixture into the ice cream so it's well distributed but still in streaks.

Transfer to freezer-safe containers and freeze until firm, at least 6 hours or for up to 3 months. (See Freezing & Storage, page 15, for tips.)

CHOCOLATE CINNAMON ANCHO

**MAKES ABOUT
2½ PINTS**

3 cups 17% Butterfat Base (page 22)

½ cup Chocolate Mom (page 59)

1 tablespoon ground cinnamon

½ teaspoon ancho chile powder (see Note)

½ teaspoon Diamond Crystal kosher salt

One of my favorite treats in the world is drinking chocolate, specifically discs of the Mexican Ibarra or Abuelita brands melted in hot milk. In fact, my first attempt to re-create those pleasures in ice cream form was just that: those circular slabs of cinnamon-spiked chocolate churned into a fluffy scoop. Nowadays, we combine really nice chocolate, the best cinnamon we can find, and ancho chile powder—not for heat but for its dried-fruit quality, which brings out those same notes in chocolate. It's a nod to the original drinking chocolate, the chile-spiked beverage invented by the Mayans more than two millennia ago.

In a medium bowl, whisk together the ice cream base, Chocolate Mom, cinnamon, ancho powder, and salt until the cinnamon and chile powder are well dispersed.

Pour the mixture into an ice cream maker and turn on the machine. Churn just until it has the texture of soft serve, 30 to 40 minutes, depending on the machine.

Transfer to freezer-safe containers and freeze until firm, at least 6 hours or for up to 3 months. (See Freezing & Storage, page 15, for tips.)

NOTE · YOU CAN TOTALLY BUY ANCHO CHILE POWDER, BUT TO GO THE EXTRA MILE, MAKE YOUR OWN: LOOK FOR ANCHO CHILES THAT ARE NICE AND PLIABLE (BRITTLE MEANS OLD). PULL OFF THE STEMS AND SLIT THEM OPEN. SCRAPE OFF THE VEINS AND SEEDS AND DISCARD THEM. TOAST THE CHILES IN A DRY PAN OVER MEDIUM-HIGH HEAT, FLIPPING ONCE, UNTIL LIGHTLY BLISTERED AND FRAGRANT BUT STILL PLIABLE, A MINUTE OR SO. LET COOL AND GRIND TO A FINE POWDER IN A FOOD PROCESSOR, MORTAR, OR SPICE GRINDER. SIFT THROUGH A FINE-MESH SIEVE. THE POWDER STAYS VIBRANT IN AN AIRTIGHT CONTAINER IN A COOL DARK PLACE FOR UP TO 6 MONTHS.

CHOCOLATE-FRECKLED DATE SHAKE

MAKES ABOUT
3 PINTS

1   cup pitted dates

¼   cup Chocolate Mom
    (page 59)

1   teaspoon ume (plum)
    vinegar or white wine
    vinegar

1   teaspoon pure vanilla
    extract, preferably
    Mexican

1   teaspoon Diamond
    Crystal kosher salt

3   cups 17% Butterfat
    Base (page 22)

½   cup chopped (chip-size
    pieces) good dark
    chocolate (see Note)

1   tablespoon vegetable
    oil

NOTE · FRECKLING
REQUIRES AN ICE CREAM
MACHINE WITH A CHUTE
OR OPENING THAT LETS
YOU ADD INGREDIENTS
WHILE YOU'RE CHURNING.

One day, after we opened Salt & Straw's first shop in SoCal, I found myself driving through the Coachella Valley and passing sign after neon sign advertising "The Original Date Shake" or "World Famous Date Shake." As I soon found out, the shakes, essentially local dates blended with ice cream (and the occasional walnut or banana), are a hyperlocal delicacy whose deliciousness is on par with the huckleberry milkshakes of Whitefish, Montana, and the mango smoothies of Homestead, Florida. I must've tried every last one. They also got me into dates themselves, and I became particularly infatuated with the Dayri variety, which I swear has the taste and texture of chocolate ganache. That got me thinking of what a tremendous team dates and chocolate make—each one echoing notes of the other—and so this scoop was born. The common Medjool date is great in this recipe, but if you want to experience the magic of Dayri, check out Flying Disc Ranch, one of the best date growers I know, who will ship them to your door.

In a blender, combine the dates, ½ cup water, the Chocolate Mom, vinegar, vanilla, and salt and blend on high, scraping down the sides as necessary, to a coarse paste, about 3 minutes. Add the ice cream base and blend on low speed until the date paste and base are combined, another 30 seconds.

Pour the mixture into an ice cream maker and turn on the machine. Churn just until it has the texture of soft serve, 30 to 40 minutes, depending on the machine.

While the ice cream is churning, pour an inch or so of water into a small saucepan and bring it to a simmer. In a heatproof bowl that can sit in the saucepan without touching the water, combine the chocolate and vegetable oil. Set the bowl over the saucepan, reduce the heat to low, and heat, stirring occasionally, until the chocolate is completely melted, about 2 minutes. Take the pan off the heat, but leave the bowl on the pan. The chocolate will stay warm until the ice cream is churned.

Once the ice cream is ready, lift the bowl of melted chocolate from the pan and dry the bottom of the bowl. With the ice cream maker still running, pour the melted chocolate through the chute in a very thin steady stream. The warm chocolate will scatter and harden into flecks, aka freckles, when it hits the cold ice cream.

Transfer to freezer-safe containers and freeze until firm, at least 6 hours or for up to 3 months. (See Freezing & Storage, page 15, for tips.)

THE RIFFS

CHOCOLATE SORBET

**MAKES ABOUT
1½ PINTS**

2   cups Sorbet/Sherbet Base (page 26)

1   cup Chocolate Mom (page 59), at room temperature

1   teaspoon pure vanilla extract

½   teaspoon Diamond Crystal kosher salt

If you ask me, the best chocolate sorbet in the world is at Berthillon, in Paris. For a solid decade, I made it my mission to crack the code, and what got me closest was tinkering with the cocoa powder. You do NOT have to go this wild, but when we mixed two parts Valrhona Dutch-process with one part natural-process TCHO brand powder, we cheered. It was just the right combo of roasty, fudgy, and fruity.

In a medium bowl, stir together the sorbet base, Chocolate Mom, 1 cup water, the vanilla, and salt.

Pour the mixture into an ice cream maker and turn on the machine. Churn just until it has the texture of a slushie, 20 to 30 minutes, depending on the machine.

Transfer to freezer-safe containers and freeze until firm, at least 6 hours or for up to 3 months. (See Freezing & Storage, page 15, for tips.)

COCOA NIB ALMOND
FRANGIPANE

CHOCOLATE SORBET

FIG & SESAME BUTTER CUP

THE RIFFS

FRECKLED MINT CHOCOLATE CHIP

MAKES ABOUT 2 PINTS

3   cups Vegan Coconut Base (page 27)

1   drop peppermint oil

7   to 8 drops green food coloring (optional)

½   cup chopped (chip-size pieces) good dark chocolate

1   tablespoon vegetable oil

NOTE · FRECKLING REQUIRES AN ICE CREAM MACHINE WITH A CHUTE OR OPENING THAT LETS YOU ADD INGREDIENTS WHILE YOU'RE CHURNING.

Mint chip is so many people's favorite scoop, but I must admit it's far from mine. It *sounds* fantastic, but to me, the typical mint chip is slightly out of whack. The bold flavor of mint steamrolls the subtle delights of dairy, with the chocolate flavor only entering the picture as the mint fades—again, it's those dang waxy chips that take so long to melt and release their flavor. Not here. First off, we apply our freckling technique, so the chocolate scatters throughout the scoop in itty-bitty fragments that liquefy upon contact with your tongue. And second, we look to coconuts, not cows, to provide a formidable counterpart to the mint. For that mint, we prefer mint oil to extract. The latter is steeped in alcohol, while the former is wrung directly from the leaves, for an unsullied flavor.

Note that freckling requires an ice cream machine with a chute or opening that lets you add ingredients while you're churning.

In the bowl of an ice cream maker, combine the coconut base, peppermint oil, and food coloring (if using) and turn on the machine. Churn just until the ice cream has the texture of soft serve, 30 to 40 minutes, depending on the machine.

While the ice cream is churning, pour an inch or so of water into a small saucepan and bring it to a simmer. In a heatproof bowl that can sit in the saucepan without touching the water, combine the chocolate and vegetable oil. Set the bowl over the saucepan, reduce the heat to low, and heat, stirring occasionally, until the chocolate is completely melted, about 2 minutes. Take the pan off the heat but leave the bowl on the pan. The chocolate will stay warm until the ice cream is churned.

When the ice cream is ready, lift the bowl of melted chocolate from the pan and dry the bottom of the bowl. With the machine still running, pour the melted chocolate through the chute in a very thin, steady stream. The warm chocolate will scatter and harden into flecks, aka freckles, when it hits the cold ice cream.

Transfer to freezer-safe containers and freeze until firm, at least 6 hours or for up to 3 months. (See Freezing & Storage, page 15, for tips.)

COCOA NIB ALMOND FRANGIPANE

**MAKES ABOUT
3 PINTS**

3   cups 17% Butterfat
     Base (page 22)

¾   cup Salted Caramel
     Syrup (page 159)

2   tablespoons cocoa
     nibs (opposite)

¾   cup Almond Frangipane
     Swirl (opposite)

The bitter edge of salted caramel and swirls of frangipane (essentially almond-y pastry cream) would make a fantastic flavor on their own, but in this scoop, they're just the stage for cocoa nibs. Cocoa nibs are just cacao beans after they've been roasted and cracked into bits before they're later pulverized and "conched" to produce the smooth, emulsified mixture used to make chocolate. Ah, but the crunch and bitter, brash flavor of nibs, which they sacrifice during the heat produced during conching, is worth celebrating. The sweetness of the frangipane balances the bitterness, so you can experience the best of the nibs' complex flavors.

In a medium bowl, whisk together the ice cream base and caramel syrup until smooth.

Pour the mixture into an ice cream maker and turn on the machine. Churn just until the ice cream has the texture of soft serve, 30 to 40 minutes, depending on the machine.

Use a spoon or flexible spatula to gently fold the cocoa nibs into the ice cream so they're well distributed. Quickly alternate spooning layers of the ice cream and drizzling on a generous dollop of frangipane into freezer-safe containers.

Freeze until firm, at least 6 hours or for up to 3 months. (See Freezing & Storage, page 15, for tips.)

ALMOND FRANGIPANE SWIRL

MAKES ABOUT 1 CUP

4 tablespoons almond paste, roughly chopped into ½-inch pieces

3 tablespoons almond flour

1 tablespoon very finely chopped roasted almonds

¾ teaspoon Diamond Crystal kosher salt

⅛ teaspoon almond extract

¼ cup confectioners' sugar, sifted

½ cup heavy cream

In a stand mixer fitted with the paddle, combine the almond paste, almond flour, chopped almonds, salt, and almond extract and mix on low speed until the mixture is crumbly and the almond paste is in pea-size pieces, about 2 minutes.

Add the confectioners' sugar one-third at a time, mixing for 1 minute after each addition. Add the heavy cream and mix on medium-high speed until light in color and slightly fluffy, about 2 minutes more.

Chill the mixture for at least 2 hours. It keeps in an airtight container in the fridge for up to 1 week.

NOTE · REALLY SPECIAL COCOA NIBS TAKE SOME SEEKING OUT. THE PRODUCT SOLD IN THE NATURAL FOODS SECTION OF GROCERY STORES IS TYPICALLY MORE ABOUT SUPERFOOD STATUS THAN FLAVOR. SO TRY THIS: LOCATE A GREAT LOCAL BEAN-TO-BAR CHOCOLATE MAKER AND SEE IF THEY'LL SELL YOU A BAG OF NIBS. A LITTLE GOES A LONG WAY, AS YOU'LL SEE WHEN YOU MAKE THIS FLAVOR.

FIG & SESAME BUTTER CUP

MAKES ABOUT
3 PINTS

3 cups 17% Butterfat Base (page 22)

¼ cup Chocolate Mom (page 59)

1 teaspoon Diamond Crystal kosher salt

¼ teaspoon ground green cardamom

1 cup Sesame Butter Cups (opposite)

¾ cup fig spread or jam (Dalmatia is my favorite), stirred to loosen

I grew up with familiar ideas about tasty partners for chocolate—you know, peanut butter and pretzels, strawberries and raspberries. So when we partnered with Diana Malouf, the founder of Los Angeles chocolatier Ococoa, I was beguiled by her chocolate reference points, which were shaped by her Lebanese heritage. For her, chocolate brought to mind fig and sesame, so our flavor collab included streaks of jam, showcasing the fruit's notes of honey and caramel, and chunks of homemade Reese's filled with tahini.

In the bowl of an ice cream maker, combine the ice cream base, Chocolate Mom, salt, and cardamom and turn on the machine. Churn just until it has the texture of soft serve, 30 to 40 minutes, depending on the machine.

Use a spoon or flexible spatula to gently fold the sesame butter cup pieces into the ice cream so they're well distributed. Quickly alternate spooning layers of the ice cream with dollops of the fig spread in thick swirls into freezer-safe containers.

Freeze until firm, at least 6 hours or for up to 3 months. (See Freezing & Storage, page 15, for tips.)

SESAME BUTTER CUPS

**MAKES ABOUT
4 CUPS BITE-SIZE PIECES**

1¾ cups chopped
(chip-size pieces)
good dark chocolate

½ cup heavy cream

1 tablespoon granulated
sugar

⅓ cup well-stirred
tahini

1 teaspoon Diamond
Crystal kosher salt

Pour an inch or so of water into a small saucepan and bring it to a simmer over medium-high heat. Measure 1 cup of the chocolate pieces into a heatproof bowl that will sit on top of the saucepan without touching the water. Put the bowl over the saucepan, reduce the heat to low, and heat, stirring occasionally, until the chocolate is completely melted, about 2 minutes. Remove the pan from the heat but leave the bowl on top of the pan until you're ready to assemble the candy.

In a medium saucepan, combine the cream and sugar, stir well, and bring the mixture to a bare simmer over medium heat, stirring occasionally. Remove the pan from the heat, add the remaining ¾ cup chocolate pieces, the tahini, and salt and let sit, stirring and scraping the pan occasionally, until the chocolate begins to melt, about 2 minutes. Use a sturdy whisk to vigorously stir until the chocolate has completely melted and the mixture becomes smooth and satiny, about 1 minute.

Spray the bottom of an 8 × 8-inch baking dish with cooking spray. Cut a piece of parchment paper to fit the bottom with some overhang (to use later as handles), put it in the dish, then spray the parchment as well.

Pour about half of the melted chocolate into the baking dish and spread it out with an offset spatula or the back of a large metal spoon to evenly coat the parchment. Immediately transfer to the freezer until the chocolate hardens, about 10 minutes.

Use a spatula to spread the tahini mixture evenly over the chocolate to make a layer about ¼ inch thick. Transfer to the refrigerator again to firm up the tahini layer, about 10 minutes.

Pour the remaining melted chocolate over the tahini layer and spread it evenly. Cover the pan and store in the freezer until fully frozen, about 4 hours.

Lift the confection from the baking dish using the parchment handles. Cut the confection into bite-size pieces and store them in an airtight container in the freezer until you're ready to use or for up to 6 weeks.

CHILI CRISP CHOCOLATE PEANUT BUTTER CUP

Like the sesame butter cups in Fig & Sesame Butter Cup (page 76), this scoop channels the spirit of Reese's cups—delicate layers of chocolate filled with creamy joy—but without the perfect rounds and fluted edges. The happy surprise here is chili crisp mixed into the filling. The fat and sweetness of peanut butter tone down the heat and enhance the chili flavor. We sneak in swirls of honey marshmallow creme for an uber-decadent Moon Pie effect.

MAKES ABOUT 2½ PINTS

¾ cup Honey Marshmallow Creme (page 199) or store-bought Marshmallow Fluff

¼ cup creamy or chunky peanut butter (I prefer Skippy Natural here)

3 cups 17% Butterfat Base (page 22)

⅓ cup Chocolate Mom (page 59)

1 teaspoon Diamond Crystal kosher salt

1 cup Chili Crisp Peanut Butter Cups (recipe follows)

In a small bowl, stir together the marshmallow creme and peanut butter until mostly combined. Set the peanut butter fluff aside.

In the bowl of an ice cream maker, combine the ice cream base, Chocolate Mom, and salt and turn on the machine. Churn just until the ice cream has the texture of soft serve, 30 to 40 minutes, depending on the machine.

Use a spoon or flexible spatula to gently fold the peanut butter cup pieces into the ice cream so they're well distributed. Quickly alternate spooning layers of the mixture and swirls of peanut butter fluff into freezer-safe containers.

Freeze until firm, at least 6 hours or for up to 3 months. (See Freezing & Storage, page 15, for tips.)

• recipe continues •

NOTE • WE, LIKE SEEMINGLY EVERYONE ELSE ON EARTH, ARE IN LOVE WITH CHILI CRISP AND SALSA MACHA. BORN IN CHINA AND MEXICO RESPECTIVELY, BOTH ARE FABULOUSLY OILY CONDIMENTS INFUSED WITH THE FLAVORS OF DRIED CHILES, SEEDS, NUTS, AND OTHER AROMATICS. EITHER WORKS HERE, THOUGH DO CHOOSE A BRAND THAT GOES EASY ON THE GARLIC AND ONION, SINCE THEY MAKE PECULIAR ICE CREAM INTERLOPERS. WE LOVE FLY BY JING FOR SICHUAN-STYLE CRISP AND HOT MAMA SALSA FOR THEIR SALSA MACHA, WHICH THEY SELL AS "CHILI OIL."

AMERICA'S MOST ICONIC ICE CREAMS

CHILI CRISP PEANUT BUTTER CUPS

MAKES ABOUT
3½ CUPS BITE-SIZE PIECES

1   cup chopped (chip-size pieces) good dark chocolate

3   tablespoons unsalted butter, at room temperature

½   cup confectioners' sugar, sifted

½   teaspoon Diamond Crystal kosher salt

½   cup creamy peanut butter (I prefer Skippy Natural here)

¼   cup Chinese chili crisp (see Note, page 78)

Pour an inch or so of water into a small saucepan and bring it to a simmer over medium-high heat. Pour the chocolate pieces into a heatproof bowl that can sit in the saucepan without touching the water. Put the bowl over the saucepan, reduce the heat to low, and heat, stirring occasionally, until the chocolate is completely melted, about 2 minutes. Remove the pan from the heat but leave the bowl on top of the pan to keep the chocolate melted until you're ready to assemble the candy.

In a stand mixer fitted with the paddle, beat the butter on medium speed until it begins to appear fluffy. Turn off the mixer, add the confectioners' sugar and salt, then beat on medium until the sugar is completely incorporated, about 2 minutes. Add the peanut butter and chili crisp and beat until just combined.

Spray the bottom of an 8 × 8-inch baking sheet with cooking spray. Line it with a piece of parchment paper with some overhang (to use later as handles), then spray the parchment as well.

Pour about half of the melted chocolate onto the baking sheet and spread it out with an offset spatula or the back of a large metal spoon to evenly coat the parchment. Immediately transfer to the freezer until the chocolate hardens, about 10 minutes.

Use a spatula to spread the peanut butter mixture evenly over the chocolate to make a layer about ¼ inch thick. Transfer to the freezer again to firm up the peanut butter layer, about 10 minutes.

Pour the remaining melted chocolate over the peanut butter and spread it evenly. Cover the pan and store in the freezer until fully frozen, about 4 hours.

Lift the confection from the baking dish using the parchment handles. Cut it into bite-size pieces and store them in an airtight container in the freezer until ready to use or for up to 6 weeks.

BLACK PEPPER GOAT CHEESE GANACHE

MAKES ABOUT 2 PINTS

3 cups 17% Butterfat Base (page 22)

¼ teaspoon freshly and finely ground black pepper

¼ cup cocoa nibs (see Note, page 75)

¾ cup Goat Cheese Ganache (below)

It's no longer just one of the best Ween albums; chocolate and cheese is also an enticing ingredient combination. I've even started seeing squares of fine chocolates on restaurants' fancy cheese plates in lieu of the typical pairings. After all, chocolate can have so many cheese-friendly flavor notes, from almond and honey to wine and dried fruit. This particular flavor was inspired by a confection from our friends at Alma Chocolate in Portland. The goat cheese acts like fresh cream in classic ganache but brings extra acidity and a bit of the barnyard. The pepper—fruity, single-origin, freshly ground black peppercorns are best here, so visit your local spice store—brings spicy berry flavor notes that amplify the chocolatey-ness so it shines through the cheese's tang.

In the bowl of an ice cream maker, combine the ice cream base and black pepper and turn on the machine. Churn just until the mixture has the texture of soft serve, 30 to 40 minutes, depending on the machine.

Stir in the cocoa nibs so they're well distributed. Alternate spooning layers of the ice cream mixture and a few dollops of the ganache into freezer-safe containers.

Freeze until firm, at least 6 hours or for up to 3 months. (See Freezing & Storage, page 15, for tips.)

GOAT CHEESE GANACHE

MAKES ABOUT 1 CUP

½ cup (about 4 ounces) fresh goat cheese (chèvre), at room temperature

¼ cup whole milk

1 cup chopped (chip-size pieces) good dark chocolate

1 teaspoon Diamond Crystal kosher salt

In a medium bowl, whisk together the goat cheese and milk until mostly smooth. Set aside.

Pour an inch or so of water into a small saucepan and bring it to a simmer. In a heatproof bowl that can sit in the saucepan without touching the water, combine the chocolate chips and salt. Put the bowl over the saucepan, reduce the heat to low, and cook, stirring occasionally, until the chocolate is completely melted, about 2 minutes.

Use a sturdy whisk to vigorously stir the goat cheese slurry into the chocolate until the mixture has completely melted and becomes smooth, about 1 minute. The ganache might have a touch of grainy texture from the cheese, which is totally okay. Congratulations, you just made ganache!

Transfer the ganache to an airtight container and store in the refrigerator until it sets up to a fudge-like texture, at least 2 hours or up to 1 month. Use it straight from the fridge.

STRAW

BERRY

You know you're a classic when you're in the Neapolitan ice cream trinity along with superstars like chocolate and vanilla. Yet do you ever get the feeling, while taking icy, refreshing licks of those pale pink scoops, that strawberry ice cream could taste a lot more like, I don't know, strawberry?

I call it The Strawberry Problem, though it applies to blueberries, peaches, and really just about any ingredient, fruit or not, with a delicate flavor that you turn into ice cream. I'm not talking sweetness or acidity, but actual strawberry-ness. You see, the more fat you add, the more luscious the texture, but the less you can make out the very thing you set out to capture in creamy frozen form. Whatever you call the problem, this chapter is full of delicious solutions. The first is an argument for promoting strawberry gelato to the prime position currently held by strawberry ice cream, and the rest are exciting and surprising ways to revel in the fruit's brief, bountiful season.

STRAWBERRY GELATO 88

STRAWBERRY COCONUT
WATER SHERBET (V) 90

AVOCADO & STRAWBERRY JAM 91

STRAWBERRY CUCUMBER
SORBET (V) 92

STRAWBERRY TRES LECHES 94

WILD-FORAGED BERRY SLAB PIE 96

ROASTED STRAWBERRIES
WITH JAPANESE WHISKEY 99

STRAWBERRIES & SOUR CREAM 101

STRAWBERRY CHEESECAKE 102

OUR ULTIMATE

STRAWBERRY GELATO

MAKES ABOUT
2 PINTS

1   pint strawberries
    (about 12 ounces),
    hulled and cut into
    ¼-inch pieces

2   tablespoons fresh
    lime juice

¼   cup granulated sugar

⅛   teaspoon Diamond
    Crystal kosher salt

3   cups Gelato Base
    (page 25)

If running Salt & Straw has taught me anything, it's that there are no right answers. Even classic strawberry ice cream—its high fat content delivering a super-creamy texture while dulling the flavor of the fruit—has its place. Ah, but what if we took all the palate-stultifying fat away? Then you'd have strawberry sorbet, which is probably the closest experience in the frozen dessert world to enjoying the platonic ideal of the fruit itself. Yet without any fat to hold the flavor on your palate, it's gone in seconds. And that's part of sorbet's charm—the flavor disappears, you want it back, so you go in for yet another spoonful.

Here we find delicious middle ground. To maintain the lickability we love in the classic while letting the strawberry flavor shine through, we settled in gelato territory, where the fat content clocks in at around 8% or 9%, about halfway between sorbet (0%) and our ice cream (17%). This means the flavor hits your palate sooner than in ice cream and sticks around longer. Plus, since fat helps trap air during the churning process, gelato's lower fat content means a denser scoop and a higher flavor per lick (or FPL, an acronym I just made up). Another bonus: Gelato is scoopable at a slightly higher temperature than ice cream. If you serve it at typical ice cream temp (about 5°F), you'd need a chisel rather than a spoon. Yet at 15°F, the texture is velvety and the gelato melts quickly on your tongue, so you get an explosion of strawberry flavor.

Into our dialed-in gelato base we blend strawberries that have been macerated (aka tossed and left to sit) with sugar and lime juice to enhance their flavor. But perhaps most important, we don't use any old strawberries: They need to be fragrant, juicy, and in-season. For so long, creamy frozen treats have been a repository for lackluster fruit. And while sugar and cream do help, never underestimate the contributions of the unique, hard-to-describe flavors of a perfect strawberry.

In a medium bowl, combine the strawberries, lime juice, sugar, and salt, toss well, and let it hang out for 15 minutes or so.

Pour the gelato base into the bowl and use a stick blender (or transfer to a stand blender) to blend until mostly smooth, about 30 seconds.

Pour the mixture into an ice cream maker and turn on the machine. Churn just until the gelato has the texture of a slushie, 20 to 30 minutes, depending on the machine.

Transfer to freezer-safe containers and freeze until firm, at least 6 hours or for up to 3 months. (See Freezing & Storage, page 15, for tips.)

THE RIFFS

STRAWBERRY COCONUT WATER SHERBET

MAKES ABOUT 2½ PINTS

1   pint strawberries, hulled and roughly chopped

¾   cup granulated sugar

1   cup pure coconut water

2   cups Vegan Coconut Base (page 27)

⅛   teaspoon malic acid (optional)

This flavor is a personal fave that almost never comes off the menu. Coconut cream for a little body, coconut water for a quiet, aromatic backdrop, and 2 heaping cups of the best berries you've got—raspberries, marionberries, or best of all, strawberries. To drive home the sweet-tart pleasure—the tart part a common casualty of the typical strawberry ice cream—we reach for malic acid. The potent white powder, which is what gives Warhead candies their wallop, mimics the acidic profile particular to strawberries, so each lick practically bursts with juicy berry goodness. It's easy to find at home-brew shops and on the internet.

In a medium bowl, combine the strawberries and sugar and let them macerate for about 5 minutes. Add the coconut water and coconut base and use a stick blender (or transfer to a stand blender) to blend until smooth. If using malic acid, stir it in right before you churn.

Pour the mixture into an ice cream maker and turn on the machine. Churn just until the sherbet has the texture of a pourable frozen smoothie, 25 to 35 minutes, depending on the machine.

Transfer to freezer-safe containers and freeze until firm, at least 6 hours or for up to 3 months. (See Freezing & Storage, page 15, for tips.)

AVOCADO & STRAWBERRY JAM

**MAKES ABOUT
1½ PINTS**

1   large ripe Hass avocado, halved and pitted

2   teaspoons fresh lime juice

1   teaspoon Diamond Crystal kosher salt

¼   teaspoon ground cardamom

3   cups 17% Butterfat Base (page 22)

¾   cup strawberry jam (see Note), stirred to loosen

One of our top tactics for bypassing the berry bind is jam-ifying fruit. When you cook strawberries with a lot of sugar, not only do you intensify their flavor, but you make them virtually unfreezable. That means strawberry floods your taste buds first. The ice cream melts next, releasing its flavor. Anything strawberry-friendly works—vanilla, basil, chocolate—but because bending minds is our forte, we opt for avocado, which has the lush fat that strawberry flavor needs to explode on your tongue. The strawberry, in turn, offers berry-rific acidity that, along with a touch of lime and cardamom, coaxes out avocado's subtle "green" flavor.

Scoop the avocado into a food processor, add the lime juice, salt, and cardamom and process until smooth. In a medium bowl, whisk together the ice cream base and avocado puree.

Pour the mixture into an ice cream maker and turn on the machine. Churn just until the mixture has the texture of soft serve, 30 to 40 minutes, depending on the machine.

Alternate spooning layers of the ice cream and generous swirls of the jam into freezer-safe containers.

Freeze until firm, at least 6 hours or for up to 3 months. (See Freezing & Storage, page 15, for tips.)

NOTE · HOMEMADE JAM IS FAB, BUT SO IS STORE-BOUGHT. FOR THIS APPLICATION, LOOK FOR TIGHTER JAMS—THOSE THAT DON'T MOVE WHEN YOU TURN THE JAR UPSIDE DOWN—SINCE THEY TEND TO FREEZE INTO MORE DISTINCT RIBBONS FOR A COOLER LOOK AND FOR A BIGGER FLAVOR EXPLOSION. BONNE MAMAN IS A GOOD EXAMPLE AND READILY AVAILABLE.

THE RIFFS

STRAWBERRY CUCUMBER SORBET

MAKES ABOUT 1½ PINTS

1   pint strawberries, hulled

½   medium English cucumber, unpeeled, roughly chopped

1   tablespoon fresh lemon juice

½   teaspoon Diamond Crystal kosher salt

2   cups Sorbet/Sherbet Base (page 26)

Sorbet is such a tease. It tantalizes you with big, vivid flavor, but without fat to help that flavor last on your palate, the smack of strawberry disappears. And that's not necessarily a bad thing. Often, on a hot day, that's exactly what I want, each lovely cold lick inspiring the next. Cucumber steps in to provide fresh green flavor that dances in the same part of your palate as the strawberry, turning this into a spa day in a sorbet.

The pairing is perfect, but take note that you can swap out virtually any combination of gorgeous fruit (plums, cherries, raspberries, peaches) and vegetable (rhubarb, beets, fennel, spinach). If they sound good together, then blend, strain, and churn. You could even buy and use good freshly pressed juice.

In a blender, puree the strawberries, cucumber, lemon juice, salt, and 1 tablespoon cold water to a smoothie texture. Strain through a fine-mesh sieve into a medium bowl, pressing (then discarding) the solids to extract as much juice as possible. Stir in the sorbet base.

Pour the mixture into an ice cream maker and turn on the machine. Churn just until the sorbet has the texture of a slushie, 20 to 30 minutes, depending on the machine.

Transfer to freezer-safe containers and freeze until firm, at least 6 hours or for up to 3 months. (See Freezing & Storage, page 15, for tips.)

STRAWBERRY TRES LECHES

MAKES ABOUT 4 PINTS

1   pint strawberries, hulled and roughly chopped

½   cup lightly packed light brown sugar

⅛   teaspoon Diamond Crystal kosher salt

3   cups 17% Butterfat Base (page 22)

⅛   teaspoon malic acid, or 2 teaspoons lime juice

    One 3-inch square Vanilla Tres Leches Cake (opposite), thoroughly smooshed

¾   cup your favorite strawberry jam, stirred to loosen

Strawberry shortcake, meet strawberry soaked-cake. The fruit shows up in the ice cream itself, roasted to intensify its flavor, and in the swirls of jam throughout each scoop. A classic tres leches cake makes a divine mix-in: Because it's soaked in milk (count 'em, three types), the cake has a similar H_2O content as the ice cream and minimizes water migration—meaning that the cake stays as light, moist, and fluffy in the pint as it was when you made it.

Preheat the oven to 375°F. Line a sheet pan with parchment paper.

On the lined sheet pan, toss the strawberries with the brown sugar and salt and spread them in an even layer.

Roast until the strawberries release their juice and begin to caramelize around the edges of the sheet pan, about 20 minutes. Transfer it all (every last bit!) to a bowl or container and refrigerate until well chilled.

In a medium bowl, combine the strawberry mixture and ice cream base and use a stick blender (or transfer to a stand blender) to blend until smooth.

Pour the mixture into an ice cream maker, add the malic acid, and turn on the machine. Churn just until the ice cream has the texture of soft serve, 30 to 40 minutes, depending on the machine.

Quickly alternate spooning layers of the ice cream, tablespoon-size dollops of the cake, and scant tablespoons of the jam into freezer-safe containers.

Freeze until firm, at least 6 hours or for up to 3 months. (See Freezing & Storage, page 15, for tips.)

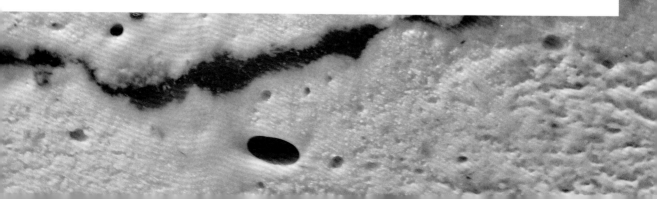

VANILLA TRES LECHES CAKE

MAKES ONE 9 × 9-INCH PAN
(8 SERVINGS PLUS ENOUGH
FOR 4 PINTS OF ICE CREAM)

CAKE

- 3 tablespoons unsalted butter
- ½ cup whole milk
- ¾ cup all-purpose flour
- 1 teaspoon baking powder
- ½ teaspoon Diamond Crystal kosher salt
- ¾ cup granulated sugar
- 1 large egg
- 1 teaspoon pure vanilla extract, preferably Mexican

SOAK

- ½ cup sweetened condensed milk
- ½ cup evaporated milk
- ¼ cup whole milk
- 1 tablespoon coconut rum (I love Coconut Cartel Special)
- ½ teaspoon pure vanilla extract, preferably Mexican
- ⅛ teaspoon ground cinnamon

BAKE THE CAKE

Preheat the oven to 350°F. Line a 9 × 9-inch baking dish with parchment paper and spray it with cooking spray.

In a small saucepan, combine the butter and milk and set over low heat until the butter is completely melted. Set aside.

In a small bowl, combine the flour, baking powder, and salt and set aside.

In a stand mixer fitted with the paddle, beat the sugar and egg on medium speed until the mixture looks lighter in color and slightly frothy, about 3 minutes. Add the milk-butter mixture and vanilla and continue mixing until combined, another minute.

Turn off the stand mixer, add about half of the flour mixture, then mix on medium speed until the ingredients are just combined. Turn off the stand mixer, add the remaining flour mixture, then mix on medium speed until the ingredients are just combined (a few small lumps are just fine).

Pour the batter into the prepared baking dish and spread it out to make an even layer. Bake until the top looks shiny and a table knife inserted into the center comes out clean, about 30 minutes, rotating the pan front to back halfway through. Let it cool completely, about 1 hour.

SOAK THE CAKE

In a medium bowl, combine the sweetened condensed milk, evaporated milk, whole milk, rum, vanilla, and cinnamon and stir until smooth. Use a fork to poke holes all over the surface of the cake. Drizzle the condensed milk mixture evenly over the cake.

Cover and refrigerate for at least 2 hours or up to 3 days.

WILD-FORAGED BERRY SLAB PIE

MAKES ABOUT 2½ PINTS

3	cups 17% Butterfat Base (page 22)
1	teaspoon pure vanilla extract
1	teaspoon Diamond Crystal kosher salt
1	cup Puff Pastry Crust Chunks (recipe follows)
1	cup Wild Berry Pie Filling (recipe follows)

Tom LaMonte's friends call him "The Bear" not because he's a tortured chef trying to turn an old Italian beef shop in Chicago into a fancy restaurant but because he's as expert at foraging for berries as any grizzly. He's been trawling the mountains for decades, and he runs Northwest Wild Foods, one of Salt & Straw's earliest and favorite suppliers. When we get a haul of Tom's treasures, we do what no bear can: make slab pie and smash it into ice cream.

Now, sure, you can fold your favorite berry pie—whether it's made with cultivated blueberries or wild huckleberries and salal berries—into freshly churned ice cream, but this way, you get to pump up the crust-to-filling ratio. And since we make that "crust" via a puff pastry hack, it eats light and flaky in each scoop.

In the bowl of an ice cream maker, combine the ice cream base, vanilla, and salt and turn on the machine. Churn just until the ice cream has the texture of soft serve, 30 to 40 minutes, depending on the machine.

Use a spoon or flexible spatula to gently fold the puff pastry crust chunks into the ice cream so they're well distributed. Quickly alternate spooning layers of the ice cream and generous dollops of pie filling in thick swirls into freezer-safe containers.

Freeze until firm, at least 6 hours or for up to 3 months. (See Freezing & Storage, page 15, for tips.)

• recipe continues •

PUFF PASTRY CRUST CHUNKS

MAKES ABOUT 4 CUPS

1   sheet (about ½ pound) ready-to-bake puff pastry, thawed

1   large egg

¼   cup demerara sugar

Preheat the oven to 400°F. Line a sheet pan with parchment paper.

Unfold the puff pastry onto the lined pan.

In a small bowl, whisk together the egg and 2 teaspoons water until the egg is frothy. Use a pastry brush to brush an even layer of egg wash over the puff pastry. Sprinkle all of the sugar evenly over the top of the pastry.

Bake until the pastry rises to about 3 inches tall and the edges are an even golden brown, about 8 minutes, rotating the pan front to back halfway through.

Let the puff pastry cool completely, then cut into ½-inch chunks. Store the chunks in an airtight container in the freezer until you're ready to use them as a mix-in (or to simply eat them) or for up to 4 weeks. There's no need to thaw the pieces before adding them to the ice cream.

WILD BERRY PIE FILLING

MAKES ABOUT 3 CUPS

2   cups mixed wild berries, cleaned and stems picked off

2   teaspoons powdered pectin

2   tablespoons fresh lemon juice

⅛   teaspoon ground cinnamon

    A couple grinds of black pepper

1½ cups granulated sugar

In a medium saucepan, combine the berries, pectin, lemon juice, cinnamon, and black pepper and cook over medium-high heat, stirring often, until the mixture comes to a boil. Add the sugar and continue to cook, stirring constantly this time, just until the jam returns to a boil. Turn off the heat.

Let the pie filling cool to room temperature, then transfer it to an airtight container and store in the refrigerator until ready to use or for up to 2 months.

ROASTED STRAWBERRIES
WITH JAPANESE WHISKEY

MAKES ABOUT
2 PINTS

- 1 pint strawberries, hulled and cut into ¼-inch pieces
- ½ cup lightly packed light brown sugar
- 2 teaspoons white soy sauce
- 3 cups 17% Butterfat Base (page 22)
- ¼ cup your favorite Japanese whiskey
- 2 tablespoons ground genmai (aka Japanese toasted brown rice)
- ½ teaspoon Diamond Crystal kosher salt

I'm always and forever a "buy in season" guy, but *shh!* Roasting makes even supermarket strawberries taste like farmers market gems. As they roast, the water they contain goes bye-bye, a little brown sugar infuses the berries and encourages caramelization, and a splash of white soy sauce coaxes out some underappreciated darker notes like anise and molasses. They freeze like teeny popsicles in this lush ice cream with a sexy whisper of whiskey (preferably a slightly peaty, oaky one) amplified by toasted rice powder.

Preheat the oven to 375°F.

On a small baking sheet, toss together the strawberries, brown sugar, and soy sauce. Roast until the strawberries begin to shrivel and caramelize around the edges of the pan, about 20 minutes. Let them cool completely.

In the bowl of an ice cream maker, combine the ice cream base, whiskey, genmai, and salt and turn on the machine. Churn just until the mixture has the texture of soft serve, 30 to 40 minutes, depending on the machine.

Gently stir in the roasted strawberries, leaving most of the juice behind. Transfer to freezer-safe containers.

Freeze until firm, at least 6 hours or for up to 3 months. (See Freezing & Storage, page 15, for tips.)

NOTE · IN THIS RECIPE, YOU'RE CHURNING TWO DIFFERENT FLAVORS AND THEN COMBINING THEM IN CONTAINERS. IT'S EASY-PEASY IF YOU HAVE AN ICE CREAM MAKER CAPABLE OF MAKING MULTIPLE BATCHES WITHOUT REST, AND IT'S TOTALLY DOABLE IN A FROZEN-BOWL MACHINE, TOO. JUST TAKE A PAUSE BETWEEN CHURNING FLAVORS SO THE BOWL CAN REFREEZE FOR AT LEAST 12 HOURS.

STRAWBERRIES & SOUR CREAM

MAKES ABOUT
5½ PINTS

STRAWBERRY ICE CREAM

1   pint ripe strawberries, hulled and cut into ¼-inch pieces

⅓   cup granulated sugar

¼   cup bourbon

3   cups 17% Butterfat Base (page 22)

2   teaspoons pure vanilla extract

½   teaspoon Diamond Crystal kosher salt

SOUR CREAM GELATO

3   cups Gelato Base (page 25)

1   cup sour cream

1   tablespoon Diamond Crystal kosher salt

1   tablespoon fresh lemon juice

This flavor is designed to re-create one of my most vivid food memories: Grandma Malek serving me a bowl of fresh summer strawberries topped with sugar and crème fraîche. We even take care to replicate the pleasure of deciding whether each spoonful would be lots of strawberries with a little cream or lots of cream with a little strawberry. And so we essentially churn two flavors—one made with strawberries macerated with sugar and bourbon to draw out flavor, and one with tangy sour cream (like crème fraîche, but less expensive)—and freeze them side by side. It's kinda like those orange-vanilla sherbet cups some of us ate as kids, only a thousand times more delicious.

CHURN THE STRAWBERRY ICE CREAM

In a medium bowl, combine the strawberries, sugar, and bourbon and set aside to macerate, stirring and mashing occasionally, for about 30 minutes.

After macerating the strawberries, use a blender or stick blender to puree the berries to the texture of a smoothie.

In the bowl of an ice cream maker, combine the ice cream base, vanilla, salt, and strawberry puree and turn on the machine. Churn just until the mixture has the texture of soft serve, 30 to 40 minutes, depending on the machine.

Turn five freezer-safe pint containers on their sides. Transfer the strawberry ice cream to the containers, filling them halfway (sideways). Cover the containers and freeze, still on their sides, while you churn the sour cream gelato (see Note).

CHURN THE SOUR CREAM GELATO

In the bowl of the ice cream maker, combine the gelato base, sour cream, salt, and lemon juice and turn on the machine. Churn just until the mixture has the texture of soft serve, 30 to 40 minutes, depending on the machine.

Transfer the gelato to the half-empty containers with the strawberry ice cream, turn the containers upright, and freeze until firm, at least 6 hours or for up to 3 months. (See Freezing & Storage, page 15, for tips.)

STRAWBERRY CHEESECAKE

**MAKES ABOUT
2½ PINTS**

3 cups 17% Butterfat
Base (page 22)

½ teaspoon Diamond
Crystal kosher salt

½ teaspoon pure vanilla
extract

½ cup Graham Cracker
Crumble (opposite)

¾ cup Liquid Cheesecake
(opposite)

½ cup your favorite
strawberry jam,
stirred to loosen

Classics aren't born. They're made. And in the past half century, strawberry cheesecake has gone from novelty flavor to bona fide classic, with virtually every ice cream brand offering its take. We're fully on board with the lovefest: The graham cracker crumble! The strawberry swirls! Our only edit: Instead of stirring in dense nuggets of baked cheesecake, we devise a tangy, creamy, no-bake swirl by calling on our buddy gelatin.

In the bowl of an ice cream maker, combine the ice cream base, salt, and vanilla and turn on the machine. Churn just until the mixture has the texture of soft serve, 30 to 40 minutes, depending on the machine.

Use a spoon or flexible spatula to gently fold the graham cracker crumble into the ice cream so it's well distributed. Quickly alternate spooning layers of the ice cream, heaping tablespoons of liquid cheesecake, and scant tablespoons of the jam into freezer-safe containers.

Freeze until firm, at least 6 hours or for up to 3 months. (See Freezing & Storage, page 15, for tips.)

GRAHAM CRACKER CRUMBLE

MAKES ABOUT 2 CUPS

5   graham crackers

1   tablespoon light brown sugar

1   tablespoon all-purpose flour

¼   teaspoon Diamond Crystal kosher salt

4   tablespoons (½ stick) unsalted butter, chilled, cut into 1-inch chunks

Preheat the oven to 350°F. Line a sheet pan with parchment paper.

In a food processor, process the graham crackers to coarse crumbs, about 30 seconds. Add the brown sugar, flour, and salt, and pulse to mix well. Add the butter and pulse until the mixture forms pea-size crumbs, about 45 seconds.

Pour the crumble onto the prepared sheet pan, spread it out, and press on it lightly. Bake until the crumble is golden brown and crisp, about 8 minutes.

Let cool to room temperature, then break the crumble up into 1-inch pieces. Use immediately or store in an airtight container at room temperature for up to 2 weeks.

LIQUID CHEESECAKE

MAKES ABOUT 1½ CUPS

½   teaspoon unflavored powdered gelatin

½   cup (4 ounces) cream cheese, at room temperature

⅓   cup granulated sugar

2   tablespoons boiling water

¼   cup sour cream

1   teaspoon vanilla bean paste

    Pinch of Diamond Crystal kosher salt

In a small bowl, combine the gelatin and 1 tablespoon cold water, stirring lightly with a spoon to fully mix. Let the gelatin sit in the water for about 1 minute so it blooms and fully hydrates.

Meanwhile, in a stand mixer fitted with the paddle, beat the cream cheese and sugar until smooth.

Add the 2 tablespoons boiling water to the gelatin and stir until completely dissolved and the mixture is clear. If necessary, heat the mixture in the microwave in 5-second increments to help the gelatin dissolve.

With the stand mixer on low, drizzle the dissolved gelatin into the cream cheese mixture and beat until well combined, about 1 minute. Beat in the sour cream, vanilla bean paste, and salt until well combined.

Use immediately or transfer to an airtight container and store in the refrigerator for up to 1 week.

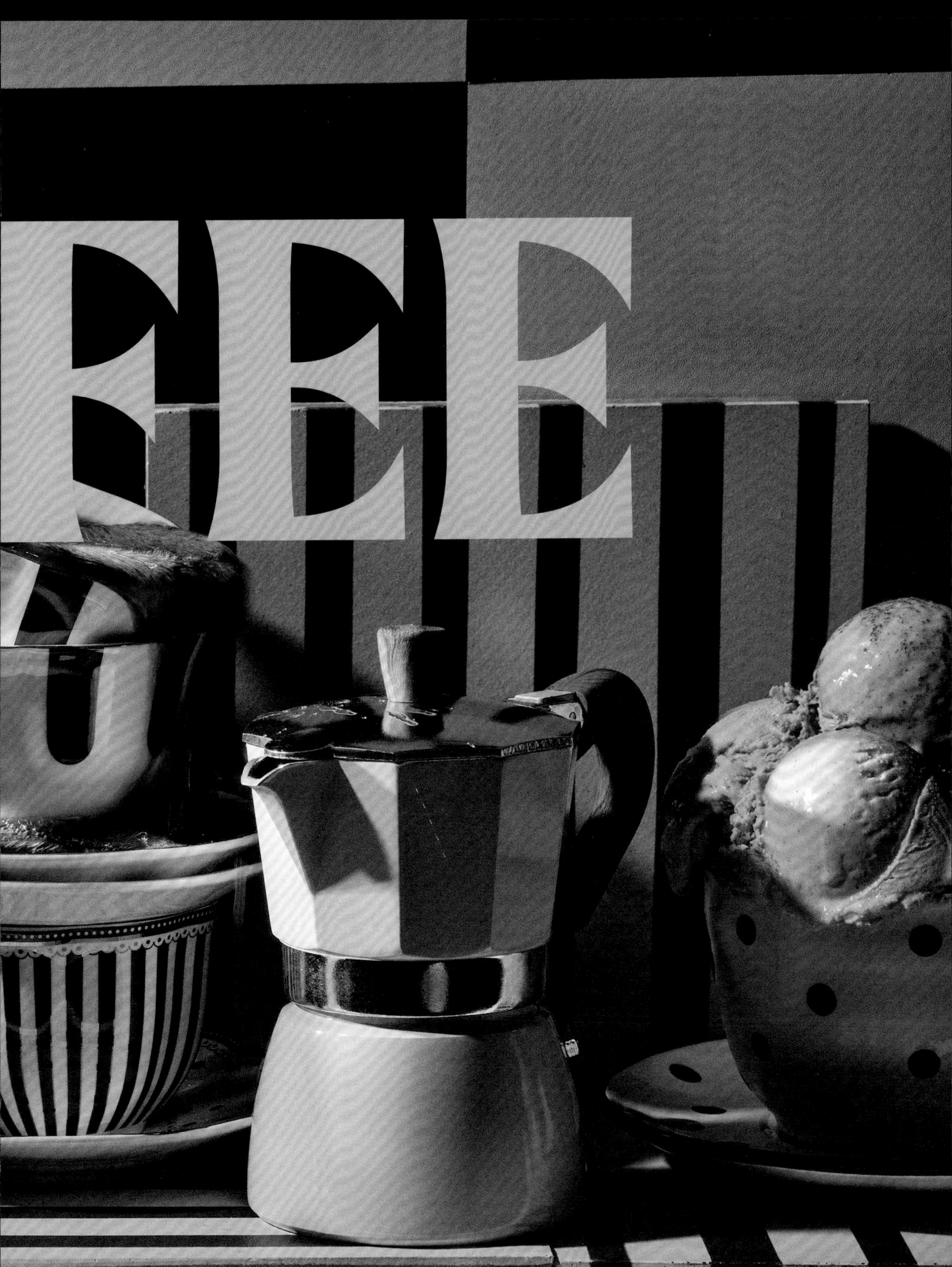

Coffee with cream and sugar is a match made in heaven. The fat grabs on to those roasty, chocolatey aromas and flavors, the sugar plays them up, and both tamp down any bitterness. No wonder coffee ice cream is one of the most beloved scoops on earth.

Of course, as the bean revolution has taught us, coffee is not a single flavor but an ingredient that's as varied and nuanced as wine. At Salt & Straw, we believe that if there's no one coffee flavor, there shouldn't be just one coffee ice cream either. That's why our version of the classic is light on its feet, giving you the ability to showcase the distinctive flavors of your favorite beans. Our riffs explore the many dimensions of coffee, looking to its besties, like chocolate and cinnamon, and unearthing some surprising pairings to open your eyes to the vast and delicious possibilities.

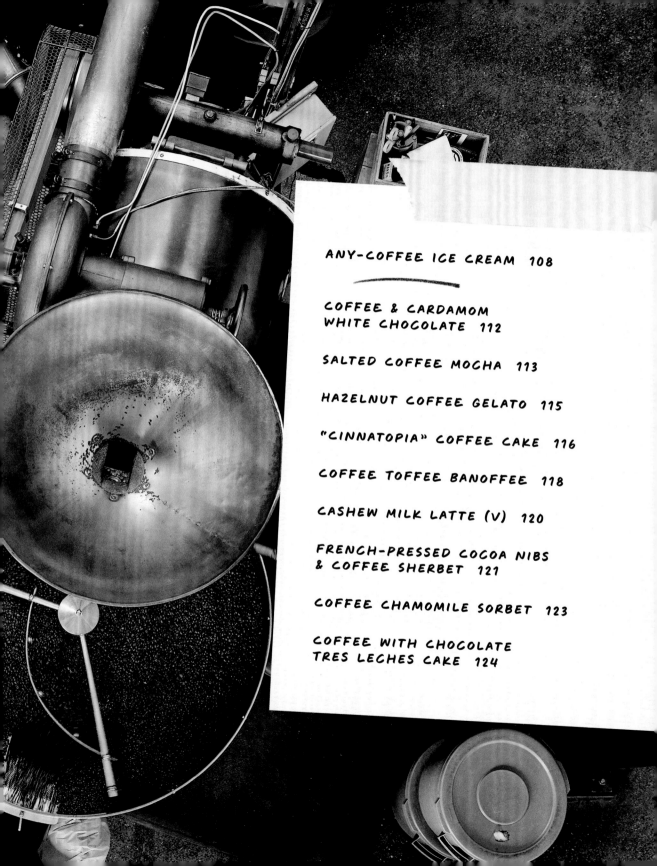

ANY-COFFEE ICE CREAM 108

COFFEE & CARDAMOM
WHITE CHOCOLATE 112

SALTED COFFEE MOCHA 113

HAZELNUT COFFEE GELATO 115

"CINNATOPIA" COFFEE CAKE 116

COFFEE TOFFEE BANOFFEE 118

CASHEW MILK LATTE (V) 120

FRENCH-PRESSED COCOA NIBS
& COFFEE SHERBET 121

COFFEE CHAMOMILE SORBET 123

COFFEE WITH CHOCOLATE
TRES LECHES CAKE 124

OUR ULTIMATE

ANY-COFFEE ICE CREAM

MAKES 2 PINTS

3   cups 17% Butterfat
    Base (page 22)

¾   cup coffee syrup
    (your choice):
    Steamy Cream-
    Immersion Coffee
    Syrup, Cold-Brewed
    Coffee Syrup, or
    Espresso-Brewed
    Coffee Syrup
    (page 111)

The question used to be, How do you like your coffee? Now the question is, What kind of coffee do you like? That familiar bitter, vaguely chocolatey profile no longer defines a cup. Instead, access to endless varieties, along with the places they're grown and the ways they're depulped, fermented, dried, roasted, and brewed, creates a universe of flavors expressed by those beans—from grapefruit to caramel, raspberry to dried fig, jasmine to licorice.

There are so many coffees to love and so many ways to take a cup.

The plentiful options are a thrill for coffee lovers as well as lovers of coffee ice cream. With a little intention, you can capture the best of your beans in your scoops by choosing the ideal method of brewing and calibrating the fat content. Four of the five main determinants of coffee's flavor—origin, variety, processing, and roasting—are built into the beans you buy, but you get to choose the method of brewing. That's why our recipe for the ultimate classic offers options: Each of the three coffee syrups uses a different method of extraction, so your scoop can reflect the best of whatever beans you buy. To choose the right one, just ask a trusted roaster or barista for guidance on the brewing method your beans deserve.

In the bowl of an ice cream maker, combine the ice cream base and coffee syrup and turn on the machine. Churn just until the ice cream has the texture of soft serve, 30 to 40 minutes, depending on the machine.

Transfer the ice cream to freezer-safe containers. Freeze until firm, at least 6 hours and up to 3 months. (See Freezing & Storage, page 15, for tips.)

ON COFFEE

THE THREE MAIN BREWING METHODS

POUR-OVER

WHAT: Hot water is, you guessed it, poured over fairly coarsely ground beans, as it is in both drip machines and manual devices such as Chemex. Thanks, gravity!

WHY: Beans with a lot of fruity, floral, herbaceous notes take well to this gentle method of extraction, which keeps those delicate flavors intact.

BEST WITH: Alas, those flavors are so delicate, they're best enjoyed in a steamy cup, not in a frozen scoop.

FULL IMMERSION

WHAT: Coarse grounds are steeped in hot or cold liquid, then strained, as in a French press or cold brew.

WHY: The boldness stands up to fat and strong flavors. Whether you're steeping with water or cream, submerging the grounds gives you a generous extraction. The fat in cream grabs onto even more flavor, including those insoluble oils that water would leave behind.

BEST WITH: It's great with spices, nuts, brown sugar, and caramel.

ESPRESSO

WHAT: Espresso machines generate a whole lot of pressure to force a small amount of hot water through fine, tightly packed grounds.

WHY: This creates a potent, viscous, ultraconcentrated extraction that includes flavors left behind by other methods—which is great for ice creams, because its intensity counteracts the palate-dulling effect of fat and the texture of the ice cream mimics espresso's rich mouthfeel.

BEST WITH: I look to pairings that lean into espresso's darker notes—think chocolate, cinnamon, and molasses—and welcome the fat content of decadent custard and ice cream.

A BETTER GRINDER

To upgrade your coffee, whether you're enjoying it hot in a mug or frozen in a cone, leave the spice grinder for spices. And not just because you want your Kenyan arabica to have notes of cherry, not notes of cumin. The real problem with these machines, some of which are sold as "coffee grinders," mind you, is that they're not ideal for . . . grinding coffee beans.

Instead, as every last coffee pro tells me, if you want to upgrade your coffee game, hold off on the fancy espresso machines and Chemex and first get yourself a burr grinder. Unlike coffee grinders with blades—which are similar to mini blenders, and you wouldn't stick your coffee beans in a blender, would you?—burr grinders use revolving wheels with little teeth to crush beans. Not only do they let you adjust the grind size, so you can easily opt for the proper grind for the brewing method you choose, but they also yield a more consistent grind—optimal for flavor extraction.

A TRIO OF COFFEE SYRUPS

These three coffee syrups use different extraction methods, each designed to maximize the flavor of whatever beans you buy. You can consult a trusted roaster or barista for tips. • *Each syrup recipe makes about ¾ cup*

STEAMY CREAM-IMMERSION COFFEE SYRUP

In a small saucepan, combine 1 cup coarsely ground (as for French press) coffee beans, ⅓ cup granulated sugar, and 1 cup half-and-half. Heat over low heat, stirring occasionally, until the mixture begins to give off steam but doesn't bubble, 3 to 5 minutes. Cover and let cool to room temperature, about 10 minutes.

Pour the steeped coffee through an extra-fine mesh sieve (or you can line a standard mesh sieve with cheesecloth or a coffee filter) into an airtight container. Press the grounds very firmly with the back of the spoon. Discard the spent grounds. Refrigerate until cold, at least 1 hour, or for up to 1 week.

COLD-BREWED COFFEE SYRUP

Combine 1 cup medium-fine ground (as for pour over) coffee beans, ⅓ cup granulated sugar, and 1¼ cups cold water in a glass jar. Seal the jar and set aside in a cool, dark place for 24 hours.

Pour the steeped coffee through an extra-fine mesh sieve (or you can line a standard mesh sieve with cheesecloth or a coffee filter) into an airtight container, pressing the grounds very lightly with the back of the spoon and then discarding them. Refrigerate until cold. The syrup will keep in the fridge for up to 2 weeks.

ESPRESSO-BREWED COFFEE SYRUP

In an airtight container, combine 3 freshly pulled double shots of espresso, ⅓ cup granulated sugar, and 3 tablespoons cold heavy cream and stir briefly. Cover and chill completely in the fridge for at least 4 hours or up to 3 days.

COFFEE & CARDAMOM WHITE CHOCOLATE

MAKES ABOUT
3 PINTS

This is our play on the cardamom-infused coffee drunk throughout the Middle East, often at family gatherings and in beautifully adorned cups. Here we make ice cream from coffee that's dark and roasty and add a touch of grapefruit zest to provide a bridge to cardamom's citrusy, floral flavor. We use two types of cardamom—green and the extra-smoky black variety—and Trojan-horse them inside white chocolate stracciatella. This way, with every lick, you first get a hit of that coffee and then a wallop of cardamom once the white chocolate melts on your tongue—a one-two punch that'll have you returning to the pint again and again.

3	cups 17% Butterfat Base (page 22)
¾	cup Steamy Cream-Immersion Coffee Syrup (page 111)
	Finely grated zest of ¼ grapefruit
1	teaspoon pure vanilla extract
½	teaspoon Diamond Crystal kosher salt
½	cup white chocolate chips
1	tablespoon vegetable oil
½	teaspoon ground green cardamom
¼	teaspoon ground black cardamom (or more green cardamom)

In the bowl of an ice cream maker, combine the ice cream base, coffee syrup, grapefruit zest, vanilla, and salt and turn on the machine. Churn just until the ice cream has the texture of soft serve, 30 to 40 minutes, depending on the machine.

When it's almost done, in a microwave-safe bowl, stir together the white chocolate chips, oil, green cardamom, and black cardamom. Microwave in

20-second increments, stirring after each one, until the chips have completely melted and formed a glossy syrup, 1 to 2 minutes total. Cover to keep melted until ready to use.

When the ice cream is finished churning, add the melted chocolate and briefly fold it in to form streaks that will quickly harden into shards as they cool in the ice cream.

Transfer to freezer-safe containers and freeze until firm, at least 6 hours or for up to 3 months. (See Freezing & Storage, page 15, for tips.)

SALTED COFFEE MOCHA

**MAKES ABOUT
2½ PINTS**

3   cups 17% Butterfat
    Base (page 22)

¾   cup Espresso-Brewed
    Coffee Syrup or
    Steamy Cream-
    Immersion Coffee
    Syrup (page 111)

¼   cup Chocolate Mom
    (page 59)

1   teaspoon Diamond
    Crystal kosher salt

To flaunt the flavor of bold, roasty beans, we call upon two of coffee's BFFs. There's chocolate, an obvious match and the ingredient that turns a coffee into a mocha. (Pause for a fun fact: The drink we now call mocha is named for a variety of beans traded in Al Mokha, a port city in Yemen, but modeled on the Italian drink bicerin.) Then there's salt, an underappreciated partner to coffee and the ingredient that makes this flavor sing, subduing the bitter notes of the brew so the complex floral and berry qualities hit their high notes.

In the bowl of an ice cream maker, combine the ice cream base, coffee syrup, Chocolate Mom, and salt and turn on the machine. Churn just until the mixture has the texture of soft serve, 30 to 40 minutes, depending on the machine.

Transfer to freezer-safe containers and freeze until firm, at least 6 hours or for up to 3 months. (See Freezing & Storage, page 15, for tips.)

HAZELNUT COFFEE GELATO

MAKES ABOUT
2 PINTS

¾ cup Cold-Brewed Coffee Syrup or Steamy Cream-Immersion Coffee Syrup (page 111)

¼ cup unsweetened hazelnut butter

1 tablespoon hazelnut liqueur, such as Frangelico

1 teaspoon Diamond Crystal kosher salt

3 cups Gelato Base (page 25)

This iconic combo began with monks in the Alps. They understood the magic that buttery hazelnuts make with roasty coffee, grinding the nuts and brewing them along with the beans. And to think, this glorious revelation dead-ended in America when big brands leaned on synthetic hazelnut flavor to distract from deficient beans. Well, hazelnut coffee returns to its former glory in this scoop. We look to hazelnut in two forms—nut butter for the fat and flavor, and liqueur for flavor and more flavor—and choose gelato as the vehicle, because its lower butterfat content and slightly higher serving temperature allow the coffee flavor to shine.

In a medium bowl, combine the coffee syrup, hazelnut butter, hazelnut liqueur, and salt and whisk until most of the chunks of hazelnut butter are blended into the syrup. Stir in the gelato base.

Pour the mixture into an ice cream maker and turn on the machine. Churn just until the mixture has the texture of soft serve, 30 to 40 minutes, depending on the machine.

Transfer to freezer-safe containers and freeze until firm, at least 6 hours or for up to 3 months. (See Freezing & Storage, page 15, for tips.)

"CINNATOPIA" COFFEE CAKE

MAKES ABOUT
2½ PINTS

3 cups 17% Butterfat Base (page 22)

½ cup Espresso-Brewed Coffee Syrup or Steamy Cream-Immersion Coffee Syrup (page 111)

One 3-inch square Cinnamon Coffee Cake (opposite)

½ cup Cinnamon Goo (below)

Can you guess what coffee cake goes great with? That's right! Yet coffee has another delicious partner in cinnamon rolls. Anyone who adds a dash of cinnamon to their latte or enjoys Mexican café de olla knows that sharp, aromatic spice goes so well with roasty coffee. These pints celebrate this throuple—rich coffee ice cream laden with chunks of coffee cake with classic cinnamon-spiked streusel along with both cinnamon roll–style cream cheese glaze and ribbons of wondrous cinnamon goo designed to stay gooey, even after freezing.

In the bowl of an ice cream maker, combine the ice cream base and coffee syrup and turn on the machine. Churn just until the mixture has the texture of soft serve, 30 to 40 minutes, depending on the machine.

Meanwhile, cut the coffee cake into ½-inch pieces.

When the ice cream is ready, use a spoon or flexible spatula to gently fold the coffee cake pieces into the ice cream so they're well distributed. Quickly alternate spooning layers of the ice cream and drizzling on thin swirls of the cinnamon goo into freezer-safe containers.

Freeze until firm, at least 6 hours or for up to 3 months. (See Freezing & Storage, page 15, for tips.)

CINNAMON GOO

MAKES ABOUT ¾ CUP

¾ cup lightly packed light brown sugar

½ tablespoon light corn syrup

1 teaspoon ground cinnamon

1 teaspoon Diamond Crystal kosher salt

¼ teaspoon xanthan gum

In a small bowl, whisk together the brown sugar, corn syrup, 2 tablespoons water, the cinnamon, salt, and xanthan gum until completely combined. Refrigerate for at least 1 hour before using or transfer to an airtight container and refrigerate for up to 2 weeks.

CINNAMON COFFEE CAKE

MAKES ONE 9 × 9-INCH CAKE
(9 SERVINGS AND ENOUGH FOR
2½ PINTS OF ICE CREAM)

STREUSEL

¼ cup all-purpose flour

3 tablespoons light
   brown sugar

¼ teaspoon ground
   cinnamon

¼ teaspoon Diamond
   Crystal kosher salt

1 tablespoon vegetable oil

CAKE

1 tablespoon unsalted
   butter, at room
   temperature

⅓ cup granulated sugar

⅓ cup sour cream

2 tablespoons vegetable
   oil

⅛ teaspoon pure vanilla
   extract

1 large egg

¾ cup all-purpose flour

¼ teaspoon baking powder

⅛ teaspoon baking soda

⅛ teaspoon Diamond
   Crystal kosher salt

CREAM CHEESE GLAZE

½ cup (4 ounces) cream
   cheese, at room
   temperature

½ cup confectioners' sugar

¼ cup sour cream

Preheat the oven to 350°F. Line a 9 × 9-inch baking dish with parchment paper and spray it with cooking spray.

MAKE THE STREUSEL

In a stand mixer fitted with the paddle, combine the flour, brown sugar, cinnamon, salt, and oil and mix on low speed until they just come together to form a pebbly mixture. Transfer to a small bowl and set aside. Don't clean out the stand mixer just yet.

MAKE THE CAKE

In the stand mixer fitted with the paddle, beat the butter and granulated sugar on medium speed until combined, about 2 minutes. Add the sour cream, oil, vanilla, and egg and mix until combined. Stop the mixer. In a medium bowl, sift the flour, baking powder, baking soda, and salt. Add the sifted flour mixture to the mixer, then mix on low speed until just combined.

Pour the batter into the prepared baking dish and spread evenly. Sprinkle the streusel over the top and use your fingers to lightly press it into the batter.

Bake until a butter knife inserted in the center comes out clean and the streusel is crisp, 15 to 20 minutes, rotating the pan front to back once halfway through. Let cool completely, about 1 hour.

MAKE THE CREAM CHEESE GLAZE

While the cake bakes, in a clean stand mixer bowl fitted with the paddle, whip the cream cheese on medium speed until softened and slightly fluffy, about 1½ minutes. Turn off the stand mixer, add the confectioners' sugar and sour cream, then mix until completely combined.

When the cake is cool, drizzle the glaze over the cake. Cut out a 3-inch square of the cake for the ice cream, transfer to an airtight container, and keep it in the fridge for up to 1 week or the freezer for up to 2 months. There's no need to thaw before using. The rest of the cake is best stored in the fridge and eaten within a week.

COFFEE TOFFEE BANOFFEE

MAKES ABOUT 3 PINTS

1   ripe banana

1   tablespoon honey

½   teaspoon ground cinnamon

3   cups 17% Butterfat Base (page 22)

¾   cup Steamy Cream-Immersion Coffee Syrup (page 111)

¾   cup Perfect Ice Cream Caramel (opposite)

¾   cup Graham Cracker Crumble (page 103)

1   ounce very fancy chocolate, shaved with a vegetable peeler

Early in my career, I got a lesson in self-seriousness from Gabe Rucker, chef of Portland's Le Pigeon and one of the most decorated fine-dining chefs in the Pacific Northwest. We were batting around wacky ideas for ingredient combinations when he said, "If it sounds cool, it'll taste cool." Honestly? He's right. Exceptions abound, but this isn't one of them. Yet while it's obvious that the flavor of the classic British dessert banoffee goes well in ice cream—um, hello, it's basically a banana split pie—you might be surprised at how the banana brings out coffee's tropical flavors. For complementary coffees, look to beans with tasting notes like clove, nutmeg, and walnut.

Preheat the oven to 350°F. Line a small baking sheet with parchment paper.

Peel the banana, reserving the peel. Use your fingers or the back of a spoon to rub the banana with the honey, sprinkle with the cinnamon, and drape the peel back over the banana. Roast on the lined baking sheet until the peel turns dark brown and the flesh is super tender, about 10 minutes.

Let cool slightly, then discard the peel and mash the banana in a medium bowl until smooth. Add the ice cream base and coffee syrup and stir until smooth.

Pour the mixture into an ice cream maker and turn on the machine. Churn just until the ice cream has the texture of soft serve, 30 to 40 minutes, depending on the machine.

Add the caramel, graham cracker crumble, and shaved chocolate to the ice cream and use a spoon or flexible spatula to fold briefly just until well distributed.

Transfer to freezer-safe containers and freeze until firm, at least 6 hours or for up to 3 months. (See Freezing & Storage, page 15, for tips.)

PERFECT ICE CREAM CARAMEL

MAKES ABOUT 1¾ CUPS

1½ cups granulated sugar

¼ cup light corn syrup

1¼ cups heavy cream

2 tablespoons unsalted butter, cubed

½ teaspoon Diamond Crystal kosher salt

In a medium saucepan, combine the sugar, corn syrup, and ¼ cup water, and stir until all the sugar looks wet. Cover, set the pan over medium-high heat, and cook, stirring occasionally, until the sugar has completely melted, about 3 minutes.

Continue to cook, still covered but this time *without* stirring, until the mixture has thickened slightly, about 3 minutes. Remove the lid and continue cooking, still without stirring but paying close attention, until the mixture turns the color of dark maple syrup, about 3 minutes more.

Take the pan off the heat and right away (with your face a safe distance from the pan!) slowly pour in the cream, stirring the whole time.

Put the pan over medium-high heat again. Attach a candy thermometer to the side of the pan. Let the mixture simmer away, stirring occasionally, until it registers 230°F on the thermometer, about 3 minutes. Take the pan off the heat, add the butter and salt, and stir slowly but constantly until the butter has completely melted.

Let the caramel cool in the pan to room temperature, then use it right away or transfer to an airtight container and refrigerate for up to 2 weeks. Separation is normal; stir well before using.

THE RIFFS

CASHEW MILK LATTE

MAKES ABOUT 2½ PINTS

1½ cups Sorbet/Sherbet Base (page 26)

1 cup cashew milk

¾ cup Cold-Brewed Coffee Syrup (page 111)

¼ cup lightly packed light brown sugar

½ teaspoon pure vanilla extract

½ teaspoon Diamond Crystal kosher salt

While we created this flavor to show off a single-origin Ethiopian coffee with the decadence and bright berry sweetness of a raspberry Danish, the principles apply to any floral, fruity bean. A gentle extraction via cold immersion coaxes out the flavor, while a dose of nut milk brings protein for lush texture. There's just enough fat to enhance, rather than overwhelm, those delicate flavors. Any nut milk works, but cashew milk amplifies any roasty notes in the coffee.

In a medium bowl, stir together the sorbet base, cashew milk, coffee syrup, brown sugar, vanilla, and salt. It's okay if the sugar isn't fully dissolved.

Pour the mixture into an ice cream maker and turn on the machine. Churn just until the mixture has the texture of soft serve, 30 to 40 minutes, depending on the machine.

Transfer to freezer-safe containers and freeze until firm, at least 6 hours or for up to 3 months. (See Freezing & Storage, page 15, for tips.)

FRENCH-PRESSED COCOA NIBS & COFFEE SHERBET

When you steep nibs in a French press, you access their lovely raw-chocolatey profile, which works so well with dark roasted coffees, each component playing up the other and creating a new, distinct pleasure. Were I drinking this concoction, I wouldn't want it as an iced latte or iced black but with just a splash of cream—so for my scoop, sherbet it is.

MAKES ABOUT 2 PINTS

- 1 cup cocoa nibs
- 2 tablespoons granulated sugar
- 1½ cups boiling water
- 1½ cups Sorbet/Sherbet Base (page 26)
- ¾ cup Steamy Cream-Immersion Coffee Syrup (page 111)
- ¼ cup heavy cream
- ½ teaspoon Diamond Crystal kosher salt

In a French press coffee maker, combine the cocoa nibs and sugar. Add the boiling water, stir, and let steep for 10 minutes. Press down on the French press, then pour out the cocoa nib tea, reserving ¼ cup of the nibs and discarding the rest. Let cool to room temperature, then refrigerate until cold.

In a medium bowl, whisk together the sorbet base, cocoa nib tea, coffee syrup, cream, and salt.

Pour the mixture into an ice cream maker and turn on the machine. Churn just until the sherbet has the texture of soft serve, 30 to 40 minutes, depending on the machine.

Gently fold in the reserved cocoa nibs and transfer to freezer-safe containers. Freeze until firm, at least 6 hours or for up to 3 months. (See Freezing & Storage, page 15, for tips.)

THE RIFFS

COFFEE CHAMOMILE SORBET

MAKES ABOUT 2 PINTS

1   tablespoon honey

3   sachets chamomile tea
    (I prefer Meadow from
    Steven Smith
    Teamaker)

½   cup simmering water

2   cups Sorbet/Sherbet
    Base (page 26)

1¼ cups unsweetened
    cashew milk
    (I prefer Elmhurst)

½   cup Cold-Brewed
    Coffee Syrup
    (page 111)

¼   teaspoon Diamond
    Crystal kosher salt

This ice cream is a delicious reminder that coffee, like cacao, is a tropical fruit and, if treated with care, can taste delicate and floral. We look for beans with tasting notes like orchid and rose, passion fruit and raspberry, and add a touch of cashew milk to give the scoop extra body. Then we double down on those tea-like qualities with, well, tea. The chamomile blend from Steven Smith Teamaker is without a doubt my favorite tea to drink and cook with (look, there it is again on page 226!). The result is unlike any scoop you've ever had.

Combine the honey and tea sachets in a mug. Pour in the simmering water and stir. Let steep for 5 minutes. Remove the sachets, squeezing them over the mug to extract the liquid before discarding. Let cool to room temperature.

In a medium bowl, combine the tea, sorbet base, cashew milk, coffee syrup, and salt and whisk until very smooth. Refrigerate until chilled, about 30 minutes.

Pour the mixture into an ice cream maker and turn on the machine. Churn just until the sorbet has the texture of a pourable frozen smoothie, 25 to 35 minutes, depending on the machine.

Transfer to freezer-safe containers and freeze until firm, at least 6 hours or for up to 3 months. (See Freezing & Storage, page 15, for tips.)

COFFEE
WITH CHOCOLATE TRES LECHES CAKE

**MAKES ABOUT
2½ PINTS**

3   cups 17% Butterfat Base
    (page 22)

½   cup Steamy Cream-
    Immersion Coffee Syrup
    (page 111)

¼   teaspoon Diamond Crystal
    kosher salt

    3-inch square Chocolate
    Tres Leches Cake
    (opposite), thoroughly
    smooshed

On display here: the lusty flavors of dark-roasted coffee, the joy of classic drinks like café Cubano or Vietnamese cà phê đá. Steeping in hot cream gives the fat a chance to grab on to every last bit of the aromatic oils in those beans, giving the ice cream a wallop of chocolate and tobacco notes. So much so, in fact, that the scoop has this wild is-it-coffee-or-is-it-chocolate quality. We magnify this by incorporating little deposits of chocolate tres leches cake, which is great in the ice cream but also on its own topped with a scoop.

We use an extra-dark roast from Panther Coffee in Miami, though any dark-roasted beans, especially single-origin Colombian, are great here.

In the bowl of an ice cream maker, combine the ice cream base, coffee syrup, and salt and turn on the machine. Churn just until the mixture has the texture of soft serve, 30 to 40 minutes, depending on the machine.

Quickly alternate spooning layers of the ice cream and tablespoon-size chunks of the smooshed cake into freezer-safe containers.

Freeze until firm, at least 6 hours or for up to 3 months. (See Freezing & Storage, page 15, for tips.)

CHOCOLATE TRES LECHES CAKE

MAKES ONE 9 × 9-INCH CAKE (8 SERVINGS PLUS ENOUGH FOR 2½ PINTS OF ICE CREAM)

CAKE

- ¾ cup all-purpose flour
- ⅓ cup unsweetened cocoa powder
- ½ teaspoon baking powder
- ½ teaspoon baking soda
- ¼ teaspoon Diamond Crystal kosher salt
- ¾ cup granulated sugar
- ¼ cup vegetable oil
- 1 large egg
- ½ cup whole milk

SOAK

- ½ cup sweetened condensed milk
- ½ cup evaporated milk
- ¼ cup whole milk
- 1 tablespoon coconut rum (I love Coconut Cartel Special)
- ½ teaspoon pure vanilla extract, preferably Mexican
- ⅛ teaspoon ground cinnamon

Preheat the oven to 350°F. Line a 9 × 9-inch baking dish with parchment paper and spray it with cooking spray.

MAKE THE CAKE

In a medium bowl, combine the flour, cocoa powder, baking powder, baking soda, and salt and lightly whisk to break up any clumps.

In a stand mixer fitted with the paddle, beat the sugar, oil, and egg until the mixture looks lighter in color and slightly frothy, about 3 minutes.

Stop the mixer, add about half of the flour mixture, then mix on medium speed until the ingredients are just combined. Add the milk and mix until the ingredients are just combined. Stop the mixer, add the remaining flour mixture, then mix on medium speed until the ingredients are just combined (a few small lumps are just fine).

Pour the batter into the prepared baking dish and spread it out to make an even layer.

Bake until the top looks shiny and a butter knife inserted in the center comes out clean, about 30 minutes, rotating the pan front to back halfway through. Let it cool completely, about 1 hour.

MAKE THE SOAK

In a medium bowl, combine the sweetened condensed milk, evaporated milk, whole milk, rum, vanilla, and cinnamon and stir until smooth. Poke the surface of the cake all over with a fork, then drizzle the mixture evenly over the cake. Cover and store in the refrigerator for at least 2 hours or up to 3 days.

cookie

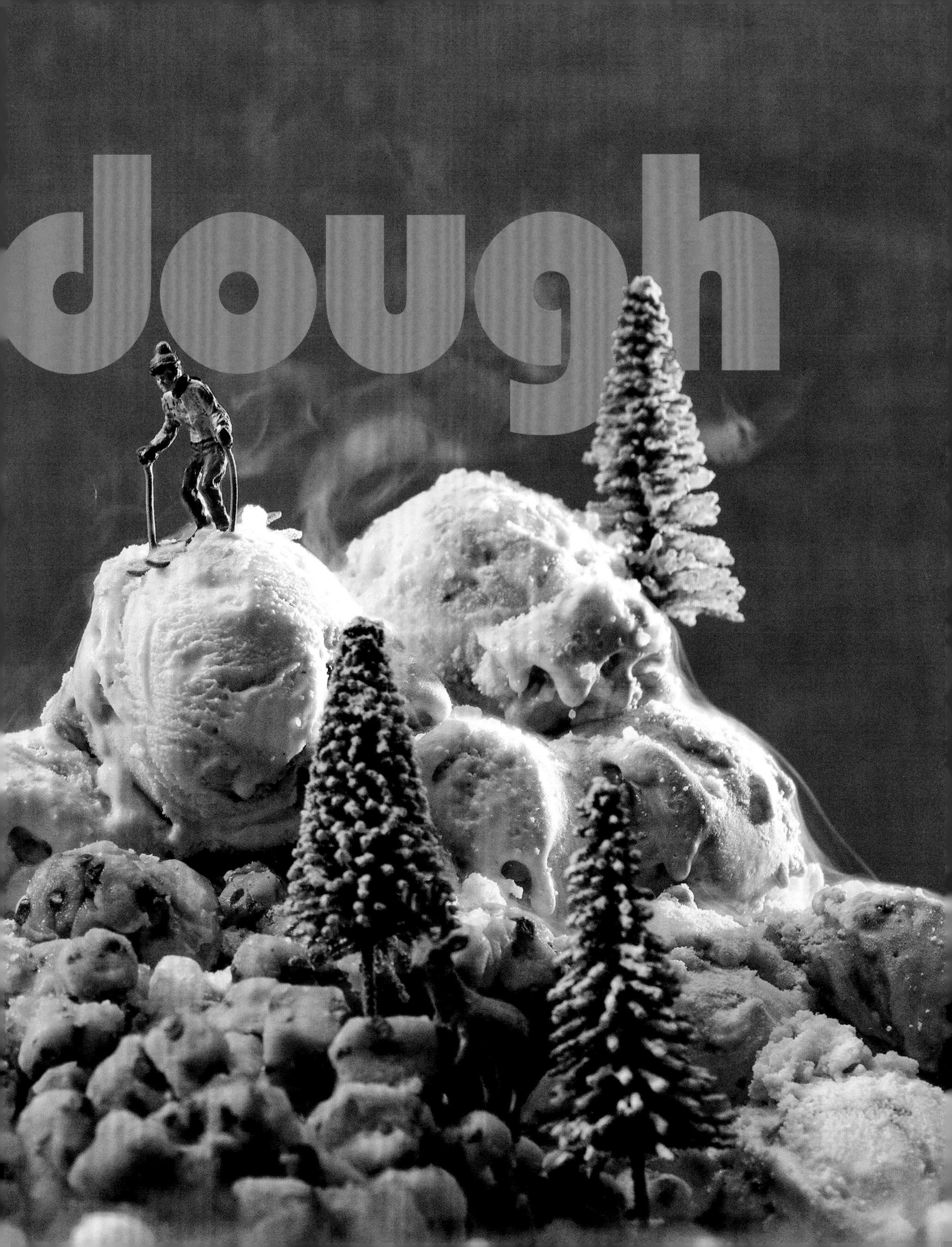
dough

As the lore goes, this epic flavor took shape around 1984 when a six-year-old upstart company called Ben & Jerry's took a customer suggestion, bringing together two of the greatest guilty pleasures, with oops-I-ate-the-whole-pint joining forces with let-me-lick-the-spoon. The key to doing the combo justice—and for incorporating the joys of any baked (or, as it were, unbaked) goods into ice cream—is anticipating the effect of freezing. How will those chunks of cookie dough, for instance, change once they're cozied up with frozen cream? The good news is we've done the work, and now you get to apply our tasty wisdom. So first, you'll find the recipe for the best cookie dough ice cream you've ever had, then you'll find more delicious ways to explore in scoop form everything from pie to pretzels to cookies to crackers.

SALTED MALTED CHOCOLATE CHIP DOUGH   130

SALTED PRETZEL ICE CREAM   134

LEMON ZEST & VANILLA MERINGUES   137

TOASTED COCONUT & SAMOA BUTTER   138

RITZ STREUSEL MOCK APPLE PIE   139

TOASTED SOURDOUGH, CHOCOLATE & EVOO   140

TRIPLE COCONUT CREAM PIE WITH SHORTBREAD CRUMBLE   143

HAZELNUT COOKIES & CREAM (V)   145

PEANUT BUTTER & JELLY COOKIE DOUGH   148

BROWN BUTTER RICE PUDDING   150

OUR ULTIMATE

SALTED MALTED CHOCOLATE CHIP DOUGH

**MAKES ABOUT
2½ PINTS**

3   cups 17% Butterfat
    Base (page 22)

1½ teaspoons molasses
    (not blackstrap)

2   teaspoons pure
    vanilla extract

½   teaspoon Diamond
    Crystal kosher salt

1   cup packed Malted
    Cookie Dough (recipe
    follows), frozen

¾   cup Malted Fudge
    (page 133)

To tell you why our cookie dough ice cream is out-of-control good, let me introduce you to a Salt & Straw in-house term of art: pluckability. If you've ever opened a pint, only to find that your otherwise kind and thoughtful significant other has evacuated every last bit of good stuff, then that, my friends, is "pluckable" cookie dough. Now, if you ask me, in the world of ice cream, there is no wrong way. Maybe those stones and pebbles of cookie dough evoke a nostalgic feeling. But me, I'm adamant that these not be pluckable and hard as rocks; instead, I want tender, decadent chunks that melt in your mouth—you know, like freshly made cookie dough.

Designing a recipe that achieves this requires, if I may geek out for a second, a molecular understanding of fat, freezing, and water migration. Or at least a lot of trial and error. Whoever created cookie dough ice cream surely took these pluckability principles into account. After all, they chose chocolate chip cookie *dough*, not chocolate chip cookies. They knew that baked cookies, over time, would soak up water from their creamy surroundings and take on a cookie-dipped-in-milk vibe . . . not a bad thing, but not luscious cookie dough either.

Confounding the fun is the complexity of Big Ice Cream. Back in the 1980s, cookie dough was likely made in-house and folded in. Nowadays, many major makers buy cookie dough from industrial suppliers. In order to not clog the machinery involved in high-volume ice cream production, the dough is designed to be dry, then extruded into pellets and frozen. Packed into ice cream and then further frozen, the pellets become unyielding and, dare I say, pluckable. Salt & Straw might be growing, but we're still agile enough to forsake those rules in favor of a super-tender *dough*.

At our factory, we apply a few cool tricks to make dough work in our machines—we make it, spread it, freeze it, then cut flour into it, so each piece is coated, like Italian gnudi. But at home, you just dollop it in after churning and before freezing. Our dough is carefully calibrated with just the right amount of edible antifreeze (salt and sugar) to resist solidification below 32°F and the right proportion of water to inhibit water migration, so it stays dense and creamy, distinct but not pluckable. Malt powder balances the sweetness and adds a roasty, toasty quality. Our answer to chocolate chips, which are waxy and tasteless when frozen, is fudge that liquefies the moment it hits your tongue.

In a medium bowl, combine the ice cream base, molasses, vanilla, and salt and whisk until smooth. Pour the mixture into an ice cream maker and turn on the machine. Churn just until the mixture has the texture of soft serve, 30 to 40 minutes, depending on the machine.

Alternate spooning layers of the ice cream and generous dollops of the cookie dough and fudge into freezer-safe containers.

Freeze until firm, at least 6 hours or for up to 3 months. (See Freezing & Storage, page 15, for tips.)

MALTED COOKIE DOUGH

MAKES ABOUT 1½ CUPS

4   tablespoons (½ stick) unsalted butter, at room temperature

2   tablespoons granulated sugar

¼   cup lightly packed light brown sugar

1   teaspoon flaky sea salt

2   tablespoons heavy cream

1   tablespoon light corn syrup

1   teaspoon molasses (not blackstrap)

1   teaspoon pure vanilla extract

½   cup all-purpose flour, toasted (see Toasting Flour, at right)

2   tablespoons malt powder

¼   cup finely chopped (chip-size pieces) dark chocolate

In a stand mixer fitted with the paddle, cream the butter, both sugars, and the salt on medium-high speed, scraping down the sides as necessary, until the butter takes on a lighter color, about 2 minutes. Stop the mixer and add the cream, corn syrup, molasses, and vanilla, then mix on medium-low speed until the mixture is just combined, about 1 minute more.

In a medium bowl, sift together the flour and malt powder. Add the flour mixture to the stand mixer and mix on medium speed, scraping down the bowl once, until there are no more clumps of flour (specks of malt are just fine!), about 1 minute. Add the chopped chocolate to the stand mixer and mix on low speed until it's well distributed.

Pack tightly into an airtight container and store in the freezer until ready to use or for up to 2 months.

TOASTING FLOUR

Our cookie dough excludes eggs for some just-in-case food safety assurance, since as you've probably heard, consuming raw eggs carries a minor but real risk of salmonella. What you might not be aware of is that eating raw flour does, too. So if you're someone who avoids sunny-side-ups or carbonara, consider playing it extra safe and cooking the flour for this recipe: Spread it on a sheet pan and bake in a 350°F oven for 15 minutes.

MALTED FUDGE

MAKES ABOUT 2 CUPS

⅓ cup malt powder

½ cup light corn syrup

⅓ cup heavy cream

1 tablespoon unsalted butter

2 teaspoons cocoa powder

⅛ teaspoon xanthan gum

¼ teaspoon Diamond Crystal kosher salt

¾ cup chopped (chip-size pieces) good dark chocolate

In a small saucepan, combine the malt powder and ¼ cup cold water and whisk until most of the lumps are broken up. Add the corn syrup, cream, and butter and cook over medium-low heat, whisking constantly, until the mixture comes to a simmer. Reduce the heat to low, add the cocoa powder, xanthan gum, and salt and continue to whisk until the cocoa powder is dissolved and the mixture looks glossy, about 3 minutes.

Turn off the heat, add the chocolate pieces, and let them sit for a minute. Whisk until the chocolate is completely melted and combined. Let cool to room temperature and then use immediately or store it in an airtight container in the fridge for up to 2 weeks.

SALTED PRETZEL ICE CREAM

MAKES ABOUT 1½ PINTS

3 cups 17% Butterfat Base (page 22)

1 cup salted mini pretzels

Cold-steeping was one of the first ice cream–flavoring techniques I ever tried. Thing is, butterfat is really good at soaking up flavors (think about the last time you left butter uncovered in the fridge and it ended up tasting like onions). I knew that much. But I was in culinary school, and my first attempt was with Flamin' Hot Cheetos. It was . . . terrible. But I persevered, learning to choose more wisely—chips, crackers, cookies, cereal—and learning to embrace the magic of plopping something tasty in your ice cream base and, 12 to 48 hours later, churning ice cream that tastes incredibly like that very thing. In this case, that's pretzels (with a touch of hot fudge, it is just divine!), but use this super-simple technique to go wild with Ritz crackers, Parmesan rinds, your favorite cereal (more about that on page 206). Really, anything but Hot Cheetos.

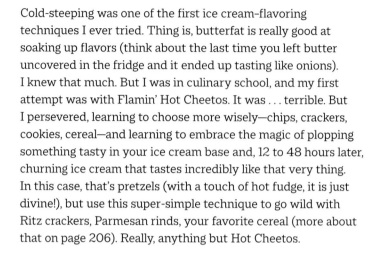

In a medium bowl, stir together the ice cream base and pretzels. Cover and let steep in the refrigerator for at least 1 hour or up to 12 hours.

Strain through a fine-mesh sieve into the bowl of an ice cream maker (discard the solids) and turn on the machine. Churn just until the ice cream has the texture of soft serve, 30 to 40 minutes, depending on the machine.

Transfer to freezer-safe containers and freeze until firm, at least 6 hours or for up to 3 months. (See Freezing & Storage, page 15, for tips.)

TOASTED COCONUT
& SAMOA BUTTER

BROWN BUTTER
RICE PUDDING

LEMON ZEST & VANILLA MERINGUES

LEMON ZEST & VANILLA MERINGUES

**MAKES ABOUT
2 PINTS**

3 cups 17% Butterfat
   Base (page 22)

2 teaspoons pure
   vanilla extract

   Finely grated zest
   of 1 lemon

1 cup vanilla meringue
   cookies, cut into
   roughly ¼-inch chunks

Water migration, it's just the worst. Until it's not. The food science phenomenon is simple—when you add something hydrophilic (that *wants* to soak up water and rehydrate) to ice cream (which is mostly water), its texture changes. Which can be a glorious surprise, when, for instance, you choose meringue cookies. They start out hard and dry, then slowly transform as they take on water, hydrating around the edges (think gooey marshmallow) while maintaining a nice crunch in the middle. It's giving, as the kids nowadays say, lemon meringue pie, which we lean into with a touch of zest.

In the bowl of an ice cream maker, combine the ice cream base, vanilla, and lemon zest and turn on the machine. Churn just until the mixture has the texture of soft serve, 30 to 40 minutes, depending on the machine.

Stir in the cookies. Transfer to freezer-safe containers and freeze until firm, at least 6 hours or for up to 3 months. (See Freezing & Storage, page 15, for tips.)

TOASTED COCONUT & SAMOA BUTTER

MAKES ABOUT
2 PINTS

6   Samoa cookies

½   cup sweetened
    condensed milk

2   tablespoons
    unsweetened shredded
    coconut

2   teaspoons light brown
    sugar

3   cups 17% Butterfat
    Base (page 22)

1   teaspoon pure vanilla
    extract

1   teaspoon Diamond
    Crystal kosher salt

Making cookie butter is a great strategy for combating the Curse of the Mix-In. Take a cookie—or pretty much any cookie-like or cake-y baked good—and puree it with enough fat and sugar to make a gooey, decadent paste, then swirl that into ice cream. After it hangs out with ice cream in the freezer, a little cream seeps in and turns the cookie butter into a dense, tender, magical bite—the kind you get when you dip a cookie in milk.

This recipe asks, What if instead of just any cookie, you use the majestic Girl Scout classic Samoa (aka Caramel deLite—same, same, different name)? Here, we make an easy toasted-coconut ice cream and spoon in our Samoa butter—all that coconut, chocolate, and caramel whizzed with sweetened condensed milk—so each lick evokes decadent coconut cream pie. Not a Samoa person? Nilla wafers, Chips Ahoy!, and chocolate cake work well here, too.

In a food processor, combine the cookies and sweetened condensed milk and process until smooth. Store the cookie butter in the refrigerator for at least 30 minutes or until ready to use.

Preheat the oven to 350°F. Line a baking sheet with parchment paper.

Toss the shredded coconut with the brown sugar and spread it evenly on the lined pan. Toast in the oven until the coconut flakes in the center are golden brown and those around the outside are a little darker, about 3 minutes. Let cool to room temp.

In the bowl of an ice cream maker, combine the ice cream base, toasted coconut, vanilla, and salt and turn on the machine. Churn just until the mixture has the texture of soft serve, 30 to 40 minutes, depending on the machine.

Quickly alternate spooning layers of the ice cream and dollops of the cookie butter into freezer-safe containers.

Freeze until firm, at least 6 hours or for up to 3 months. (See Freezing & Storage, page 15, for tips.)

RITZ STREUSEL MOCK APPLE PIE

**MAKES ABOUT
2½ PINTS**

½ cup coarsely crumbled Ritz crackers

4 tablespoons (½ stick) unsalted butter, melted

1 tablespoon light brown sugar

3 cups 17% Butterfat Base (page 22)

½ cup apple cider

1 tablespoon ground cinnamon

1 teaspoon Diamond Crystal kosher salt

As a kid, I loved Ritz crackers (sprayed with Easy Cheese, please). As an adult, I became semi-obsessed with the back-of-the-box recipe called Ritz Mock Apple Pie. Invented during the Great Depression, this genius-level innovation involves baking a crust filled with a mixture of Ritz crackers, water, sugar, lemon, and cinnamon. I know. But somehow the filling transmogrifies into a dead ringer for gooey apple pie filling.

This ice cream homage keeps things almost apple free (a little cider goes a long way) and leans into the glory of those crisp, flaky crackers, which we bathe in butter to create a fat barrier that keeps them from going soggy.

In a small bowl, stir together the crackers, melted butter, and brown sugar until the crackers are really well coated. Set aside while the ice cream churns.

In a medium bowl, whisk together the ice cream base, apple cider, cinnamon, and salt. Pour the mixture into an ice cream maker and turn on the machine. Churn just until the ice cream has the texture of soft serve, 30 to 40 minutes, depending on the machine.

Stir in the cracker mixture. Transfer to freezer-safe containers and freeze until firm, at least 6 hours or for up to 3 months. (See Freezing & Storage, page 15, for tips.)

TOASTED SOURDOUGH, CHOCOLATE & EVOO

**MAKES ABOUT
2 PINTS**

As much as we try to preimagine how a baked good will taste in ice cream, sometimes we just take a chance and blend something into the base to see how it tastes. When we tried this strategy with sourdough bread, for instance, we swooned—it tasted like creamy frozen bread pudding! Over the years, we've refined the recipe, toasting the bread a little darker than seems reasonable and embellishing the scoop with chocolate and olive oil in an ode to pan con chocolate, the classic Spanish dessert.

¾	cup cubed (1-inch) crusty sourdough bread
3	cups 17% Butterfat Base (page 22)
1	teaspoon Diamond Crystal kosher salt
½	cup chopped (chip-size pieces) good dark chocolate
¼	cup extra-virgin olive oil
1	tablespoon brown rice vinegar or malt vinegar

Preheat the oven to 425°F. Line a baking sheet with parchment paper.

Spread the bread in a single layer on the lined pan and toast in the oven until the cubes in the center are golden brown and those around the outside are a little darker, about 8 minutes.

Transfer the sourdough to a medium bowl. Add the ice cream base and salt and stir well. Let the bread soak in the base until softened, 20 to 30 minutes.

Use a stick blender (or transfer to a stand blender) to blend until mostly smooth. Add the chocolate pieces, olive oil, and vinegar and blend again until the chocolate breaks up slightly.

Pour the mixture into an ice cream maker and turn on the machine. Churn just until the ice cream has the texture of soft serve, 30 to 40 minutes, depending on the machine.

Transfer to freezer-safe containers and freeze until firm, at least 6 hours or for up to 3 months. (See Freezing & Storage, page 15, for tips.)

TRIPLE COCONUT CREAM PIE
WITH SHORTBREAD CRUMBLE

One of our most popular collaborations, this scoop was developed in concert with the folks at Dahlia Bakery, Tom Douglas's Seattle stalwart. To evoke the majesty of their famous coconut cream pie, we get a little extra with coconut (toasted flakes flavor the base and candied flakes are mixed in before freezing). We look to Honey Marshmallow Creme, which stays velvety in the freezer. And we use dense, buttery shortbread, which transforms in the freezer to provide flaky-pie-crust vibes.

MAKES ABOUT 3 PINTS

¼ cup unsweetened shredded coconut

3 cups Rich Custard Base (page 24)

1 teaspoon Diamond Crystal kosher salt

¾ cup chopped Coconut Shortbread Cookies (recipe follows)

½ cup Candied Coconut Flakes (recipe follows)

1 cup Honey Marshmallow Creme (page 199), or store-bought Marshmallow Fluff

Preheat the oven to 300°F.

Sprinkle the shredded coconut in an even layer on a sheet pan and bake, shaking the pan occasionally, until the coconut is an even dark amber color, about 5 minutes.

In a medium bowl, combine the toasted coconut, ice cream base, and salt. Refrigerate for at least 1 hour until the coconut softens.

With a stick blender (or transfer to a stand blender), blend the mixture until the coconut is in small pieces. Pour the mixture into an ice cream maker and turn on the machine. Churn just until the ice cream has the texture of soft serve, 30 to 40 minutes, depending on the machine.

Use a spoon or flexible spatula to gently fold the coconut shortbread pieces and candied coconut flakes into the ice cream so they're well distributed. Alternate spooning layers of the ice cream and generous dollops of marshmallow creme into freezer-safe containers.

Freeze until firm, at least 6 hours or for up to 3 months. (See Freezing & Storage, page 15, for tips.)

• recipe continues •

COCONUT SHORTBREAD COOKIES

MAKES ABOUT 12 COOKIES, PLUS ENOUGH FOR 3 PINTS OF ICE CREAM

8 tablespoons (1 stick) unsalted butter

⅓ cup granulated sugar

¾ cup all-purpose flour

¼ cup unsweetened shredded coconut

¼ cup cornstarch

½ teaspoon pure vanilla extract

½ teaspoon Diamond Crystal kosher salt

Preheat the oven to 325°F. Line a sheet pan with parchment paper and spray it with cooking spray.

In a stand mixer fitted with the paddle, cream the butter and sugar on medium-high speed until the butter takes on a lighter color, about 2 minutes. Stop the mixer and add the flour, shredded coconut, cornstarch, vanilla, and salt. Return the mixer to medium-low speed and stir until the mixture is just combined and slightly pebbly.

Dump the dough onto the lined sheet pan, press it together, and use a rolling pin to roll it about ¼-inch thick.

Bake until the shortbread is golden brown around the edges, about 15 minutes.

Let the shortbread cool to room temperature. Cut enough of the shortbread into small pieces (¼- to ½-inch) to give you ¾ cup, then cut the remaining shortbread into 12 cookie-size pieces. Use the ¾ cup chopped shortbread immediately for the ice cream or store in the freezer for up to 2 months. Cover and store the rest for up to 1 week.

CANDIED COCONUT FLAKES

MAKES ABOUT ¾ CUP

¾ cup unsweetened coconut flakes or shredded coconut

2 tablespoons light corn syrup

1½ teaspoons vanilla bean paste

In a small bowl, combine the coconut, corn syrup, and vanilla paste and rub them together with your fingers until the coconut flakes are evenly coated. Refrigerate the mixture until the flakes plump up, at least 1 hour and up to 4 hours.

Preheat the oven to 300°F. Line a sheet pan with parchment paper and spray it with cooking spray.

Spread the coconut mixture in an even layer on the sheet pan and bake, stirring occasionally, until the coconut is an even dark amber color, 5 to 8 minutes.

Let it cool in the pan to room temp, then transfer to the fridge and let it cool completely, stirring occasionally to break it up slightly. Store in a sealed container at room temperature for up to 2 weeks.

HAZELNUT COOKIES & CREAM

**MAKES ABOUT
2½ PINTS**

½ cup Chocolate Mom (page 59)

¼ cup unsweetened hazelnut butter

1 teaspoon Diamond Crystal kosher salt

3 cups Vegan Coconut Base (page 27)

1 cup chopped Chocolate Cookie Chunks (recipe follows) or Oreo cookies

This is a riff on Cookies & Cream, my favorite treat growing up (Safeway brand, mostly melted), a flavor so nostalgically perfect that I once thought I'd never make it myself. Vanilla ice cream would be lovely, of course, but I stray in part to keep my childhood memories sacred and in part because hazelnut and chocolate make a wildly tasty partner for Oreos. Cookies straight off the shelf totally do the trick—we love the way they slurp up liquid as they freeze—but there's nothing like making your own. And I don't mean some fancy version either—I'm talking a replica (albeit gluten-free), imitation-vanilla-spiked creamy middle and all. Make sure to source black cocoa powder for color and that distinctive Oreo bitterness. For extra credit, swap out half the black cocoa powder for red (rouge) cocoa powder, which is not quite as alkalized as black and provides some welcome balance.

In a medium bowl, combine the Chocolate Mom, hazelnut butter, and salt and whisk until the hazelnut butter thins out into the chocolate syrup and the mixture is smooth. Whisk in the ice cream base.

Pour the mixture into an ice cream maker and turn on the machine. Churn just until the ice cream has the texture of soft serve, 30 to 40 minutes, depending on the machine.

Use a spoon or flexible spatula to gently fold the cookie pieces into the ice cream so they're well distributed.

Transfer to freezer-safe containers and freeze until firm, at least 6 hours or for up to 3 months. (See Freezing & Storage, page 15, for tips.)

• recipe continues •

CHOCOLATE COOKIE CHUNKS

MAKES ABOUT 10 COOKIES,
PLUS ENOUGH FOR
2½ PINTS OF ICE CREAM

COOKIES

½ cup gluten-free
  1-to-1 flour (I like
  Bob's Red Mill)

¼ cup black cocoa powder

½ teaspoon baking soda

½ teaspoon baking powder

⅓ cup granulated sugar

½ teaspoon Diamond
  Crystal kosher salt

4 tablespoons Earth
  Balance vegan butter,
  at room temperature

FILLING

5 tablespoons Earth
  Balance vegan butter,
  cut into ¼-inch cubes,
  at room temperature

1⅓ cups confectioners'
  sugar, sifted

¾ teaspoon clear
  (imitation) vanilla
  extract

BAKE THE COOKIES

Preheat the oven to 300°F. Line a baking sheet with parchment paper and spray it with cooking spray.

In a stand mixer fitted with the paddle, stir together the flour, cocoa powder, baking soda, baking powder, granulated sugar, and salt. Add the vegan butter and mix on medium-low speed until the mixture is just combined and slightly pebbly.

Dump the dough onto the lined baking sheet, press it together, and use a rolling pin to roll it about ¼-inch thick.

Bake until set in the center and slightly crispy on the edges, about 15 minutes, rotating the pan front to back halfway through.

Let the cookie cool completely while you make the filling.

MAKE THE FILLING

In a stand mixer fitted with the paddle, whip the vegan butter on high speed until softened, about 30 seconds. Stop the mixer, add about one-third of the confectioners' sugar, and mix to combine. Repeat until all the sugar is added, beating after each addition. Add the vanilla and mix briefly to combine.

Use an offset spatula to spread the filling onto half of the cooled chocolate cookie. Fold the unfrosted half of the cookie on top of the frosted half. It'll break but that's okay—just puzzle-piece the top half back together using the filling as glue. Refrigerate until the filling firms up, about 4 hours.

Cut enough of the cookie into ¼-inch chunks to give you 1 cup and cut the rest into cookie-size pieces. Store the chunks in an airtight container in the refrigerator until ready to use as a mix-in or for up to 2 weeks. Store the cookies the same way.

PEANUT BUTTER & JELLY COOKIE DOUGH

**MAKES ABOUT
2 PINTS**

3 cups 17% Ice Cream Base (page 22)

2 tablespoons cornflakes

1 teaspoon pure vanilla extract

½ teaspoon Diamond Crystal kosher salt

1 cup ½-inch cubes Peanut Butter Cookie Dough (opposite)

¾ cup your favorite raspberry jam, stirred to loosen

Chocolate chip cookie dough is the classic, but it's just a starting point. And since my heart belongs to peanut butter cookies, we make a mix-in that really dials in the ratio of fat, flour, and water to achieve a decadent velvety texture after freezing. To perk up your palate, we call upon peanut butter's bestie—your favorite jelly or jam, whether that's classy (to me, at least) raspberry or nostalgic (to me, at least) grape. In the ice cream itself, a touch of cornflakes is the secret to a malty character that brings to mind the bread in a PB&J.

In a medium bowl, combine the ice cream base, cornflakes, vanilla, and salt and use a stick blender (or transfer to a stand blender) to blend until fairly smooth. Pour the mixture into an ice cream maker and turn on the machine. Churn just until the ice cream has the texture of soft serve, 30 to 40 minutes, depending on the machine.

Use a spoon or flexible spatula to gently fold the cookie dough pieces into the ice cream so they're well distributed. Quickly alternate spooning layers of the mixture and about 1-tablespoon dollops of the jam into freezer-safe containers.

Freeze until firm, at least 6 hours or for up to 3 months. (See Freezing & Storage, page 15, for tips.)

PEANUT BUTTER COOKIE DOUGH

MAKES ABOUT 2¼ CUPS,
ENOUGH FOR 4 PINTS OF
ICE CREAM, PLUS A FEW NIBBLES

4   tablespoons (½ stick)
     unsalted butter, at room
     temperature

⅓   cup chunky peanut butter
     (I love Skippy Natural
     here)

¼   cup lightly packed light
     brown sugar

¼   cup granulated sugar

1½   teaspoons flaky sea salt

½   teaspoon Diamond Crystal
     kosher salt

⅓   cup whole milk

⅛   teaspoon pure vanilla
     extract

¾   cup all-purpose flour
     (toasted, if preferred;
     see Toasting Flour,
     page 132)

Line a sheet pan with parchment paper and spray it with cooking spray.

In a stand mixer fitted with the paddle, cream the butter, peanut butter, brown sugar, granulated sugar, sea salt, and kosher salt on medium-high speed until completely combined and a shade or so lighter in color, about 1 minute. Reduce the speed to low, add the milk and vanilla, and mix until combined, about 1 minute more.

Stop the mixer and add the flour. Return the mixer to medium speed and mix until combined, about 3 minutes. Dump the dough onto the prepared sheet pan, then use a spatula to press it into an even ½-inch-thick layer. Transfer to the freezer and freeze the dough until it's hardened, at least 4 hours.

Remove the dough and cut it into ½-inch cubes. Use immediately or store in an airtight container in the freezer for up to 2 months.

BROWN BUTTER RICE PUDDING

MAKES ABOUT
2 PINTS

¾ cup basmati rice

3 cups Rich Custard Base (page 24)

2 tablespoons ground genmai (Japanese toasted brown rice; optional)

1 teaspoon Diamond Crystal kosher salt

½ cup Verjus-Soaked Currants (opposite), drained

½ cup Brown-Butter Pepitas (opposite)

One bite of the Jeweled Crispy Rice at the Los Angeles restaurant Kismet inspired us to collab with chefs Sara Kramer and Sarah Hymanson on a flavor that celebrates their savory-sweet stunner. To platform the gorgeous but subtle rice flavor, we dark-toast and then steep basmati rice, and add a little Japanese toasted rice powder for good measure. We straight-up snatch Sara and Sarah's verjus-plumped currants, and we manipulate the pumpkin seeds in their version to re-create their baked rice's crackling crust. In a nod to the two runny yolks that leak out when you crack through the crust of their jeweled rice, we opt for our extra-rich egg custard base.

Preheat the oven to 300°F.

Sprinkle the basmati rice in an even layer on a sheet pan and bake, shaking the pan occasionally, until the rice is an even dark amber color, 15 to 20 minutes.

In a medium bowl, combine the toasted rice, ice cream base, genmai (if using), and salt. Refrigerate for at least 4 hours, until the base is completely chilled and has soaked up the rice flavors.

Strain through a fine-mesh sieve, discarding the solids. Pour the mixture into an ice cream maker and turn on the machine. Churn just until the ice cream has the texture of soft serve, 30 to 40 minutes, depending on the machine.

Use a spoon or flexible spatula to gently fold the currants and pepitas into the ice cream so they're well distributed. Transfer to freezer-safe containers and freeze until firm, at least 6 hours or for up to 3 months. (See Freezing & Storage, page 15, for tips.)

VERJUS-SOAKED CURRANTS

MAKES ABOUT 1 CUP

¾ cup granulated sugar

½ cup verjus or acidic
   but fruity white wine

¾ cup dried currants

1 tablespoon champagne
   vinegar

In a small saucepan, combine the sugar and verjus and cook over medium heat until the sugar is completely dissolved. Turn off the heat and add the currants and vinegar. Transfer to an airtight container and store in the refrigerator until the currants are fully plumped, overnight or for up to 3 weeks.

BROWN-BUTTER PEPITAS

MAKES ABOUT 1¼ CUPS

3 tablespoons salted
   butter

2 cups mini marshmallows

¾ cup pepitas

1 teaspoon flaky sea salt

Preheat the oven to 325°F. Line a sheet pan with parchment paper and spray it with cooking spray.

In a small saucepan, melt the butter over medium heat, cooking it until the milk solids begin to brown, 3 to 5 minutes.

Once the milk solids get to the perfect light amber, reduce the heat to low and immediately add the marshmallows. Cook on low until the marshmallows are mostly melted, another minute; it's okay if the marshmallows and butter look a little separated. Turn off the heat.

Add the pepitas and salt and stir until evenly coated in marshmallow goo.

Spread the pepitas in an even layer on the lined pan. Spray a spatula with cooking spray to help spread and break up large clumps.

Bake the pepitas until they are dark amber around the edges and golden brown in the center, about 10 minutes.

Let cool completely. Break into bite-size pieces and store in an airtight container until ready to use or for up to 2 weeks.

SALTED CARAMEL

Soon after this irresistible flavor exploded onto the scoop scene, it became a modern classic. But not—or so my theory goes—because everyone loves salty-sweet. Instead, the magic of salted caramel ice cream is how salt and sugar interact with the true star: that epic bitterness. For our take on the classic, we lean in hard, concocting an extra-dark salted caramel syrup to ensure that this flavor comes through amid all that luscious butterfat. Our other riffs look to an array of caramel drizzles infused with burnt sugar-friendly flavors both sweet (bananas!) and savory (fish sauce and lemongrass!) and designed to stay gooey when frozen. And while bitterness is at the heart of the pleasure, salt matters, too, so I show you how to up your salt game to take these flavors to the next level.

SALTED CARAMEL 156

SALTED CARAMEL & PEANUTS
STRACCIATELLA 162

SALTED CARAMEL APPLE SHERBET 163

CARAMELIZED PINEAPPLE SHERBET
(V) 164

BANANAS FOSTER RUM CARAMEL
(V) 166

SALTED SWEET CREAM WITH
HONEYCOMB CANDY 167

SALTED CHOCOLATE CUPCAKE 170

CHOCOLATE CARAMEL POTATO CHIP
CUPCAKE 173

SALTED CARAMELIZED GRAPEFRUIT
SHERBET 176

LEMONGRASS & FISH SAUCE
CARAMEL 178

OUR ULTIMATE

SALTED CARAMEL

MAKES ABOUT
2½ PINTS

3   cups 17% Butterfat
    Base (page 22) or
    Vegan Coconut Base
    (page 27)

¾   cup Salted Caramel
    Syrup (page 159)

If salted caramel seems like a no-brainer now, you'll be surprised to learn that it's not some centuries-old French pastry tradition but rather an innovation just a bit older than the chicken nugget. It didn't exist until 1977, when a chocolatier from Brittany named Henri Le Roux swapped in salted butter for the unsalted butter traditionally used to make caramel. He used the region's specialty: butter from the cows of Brittany mixed with the salt harvested from the marshes of the nearby town of Guérande. French pastry chefs first took notice, then chefs and candymakers in the United States (Fran's Chocolates out of Seattle was an early adopter), then the floodgates opened. By the early 2000s, you could suddenly score a salted caramel latte at Starbucks or a pint from Häagen-Dazs.

The secret to our ultimate classic is a salted caramel syrup that features especially dark caramelized sugar for flavor and plenty of sea salt for balance. To find out why, see On Salted Caramel (page 158). To taste why, get churning!

In the bowl of an ice cream maker, combine the ice cream base and caramel syrup and turn on the machine. Churn just until the mixture has the texture of soft serve, 30 to 40 minutes, depending on the machine.

Transfer to freezer-safe containers and freeze until firm, at least 6 hours or for up to 3 months. (See Freezing & Storage, page 15, for tips.)

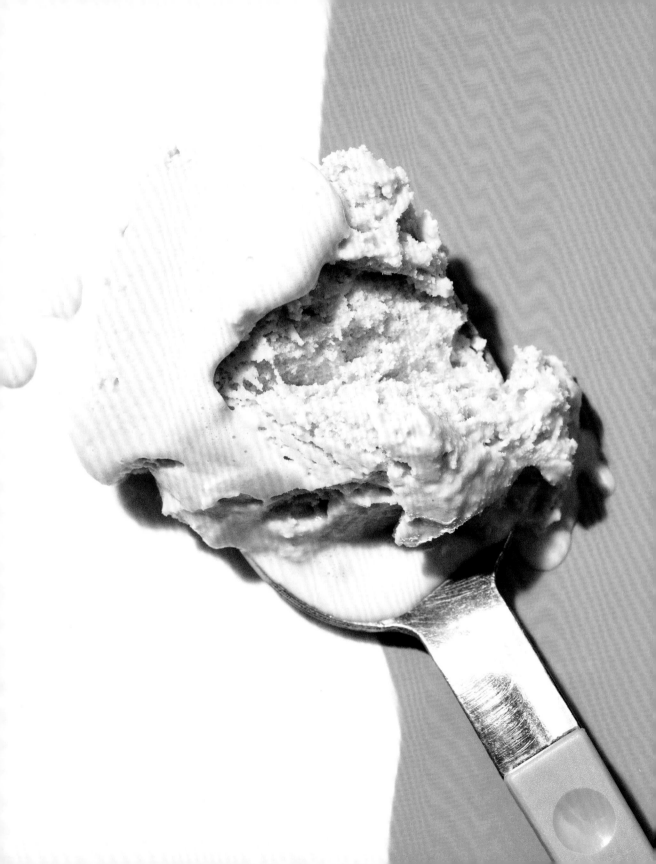

ON SALTED CARAMEL

For some, the takeaway from the idea of salted caramel is that salt could be added to sweets. But to me, the reason salt works so well with caramel (and chocolate, for that matter) is the way it highlights caramel's most intriguing quality: bitterness.

As I went from ice cream customer to ice cream maker, I dug into the science of food and flavor and found out how this works: Salt tempers bitterness by literally blocking the receptors on our tongue so they can't detect it. But lucky for us, it doesn't block them all—salt dulls the astringency that can overwhelm your palate and lets you experience all the beautiful, nuanced components of burnt sugar.

And friends, this is no time for kosher salt. As my salt guru, Mark Bitterman, showed me early on, salt is not just salt. So here I look to flaky sea salt (and, if I really want to go the extra mile, to Guatemalan fleur de sel). Because flaky sea salt often has less of the astringency you get from the high

mineral content of kosher salt, you can add almost twice as much flaky sea salt without getting those off flavors. That means less of the harsh bitterness from the caramel, a lovely clean salinity (and, if you ask me, umami) from the salt, and the pure pleasures of fat and scalded sugar.

Our first step in making salted caramel will be to make a caramel concentrate, going light on the cream (be it from a cow or, for the vegans, a coconut) and hard on the sugar to bring out all those complex notes. And I mean *hard*—you're going to have to open a window and consider turning on a fan because the sugar's going to smoke. On its own, this syrup would be too intense to enjoy, but remember: We're combating its intensity with dilution (after all, we're mixing it with 3 cups of ice cream base) and the flavor-stultifying effect that's inevitable during its alchemic transformation from cold liquid to creamy, dreamy frozen treat.

SALTED CARAMEL SYRUP

MAKES ABOUT 1½ CUPS

½ cup heavy cream or unsweetened
   coconut cream
1 cup granulated sugar
2 tablespoons light corn syrup
2 teaspoons flaky sea salt

In a cup with a spout, combine the cream
and ½ cup water. Set aside.

In a medium saucepan, combine the
sugar, corn syrup, and 2 tablespoons water
and stir until all of the sugar looks wet.
Cover, set the pan over medium-high heat,
and cook at a gentle boil, stirring occasionally, until the sugar has completely melted,
about 3 minutes.

Continue to cook, covered, but this
time *without* stirring, until the mixture has
thickened, about 3 minutes.

Uncover and continue cooking, still
without stirring but paying close attention,
until the mixture turns dark brown and
begins to smoke, about 4 minutes more.

Take the pan off the heat and, with
your face a safe distance from the pan,
immediately pour in the cream mixture in
a thin steady stream, stirring as you pour.

Set the pan back over medium-high
heat and cook, stirring constantly, just until
any sugar that has hardened has completely
re-melted, about 2 minutes. Stir in the salt.

Let cool to room temperature. Refrigerate until well chilled and for up to 2 weeks.

Fleur de Sel from Guatemala

SALT

Black Diamond Salt from Cyprus

Sel Gris from France

Sal Grosso from Brazil

Sel Gris

FROM FRANCE

SALTED CARAMEL & PEANUTS STRAC- CIATELLA

**MAKES ABOUT
3 PINTS**

3   cups 17% Butterfat Base (page 22)

¾   cup Salted Caramel Syrup (page 159)

¾   cup chopped (chip-size pieces) good dark chocolate

2   teaspoons vegetable oil

⅓   cup salted roasted peanuts, roughly chopped

For purists, a pint of our salted caramel ice cream lacks not a thing except a spoon. But for ice cream lovers craving a candy bar vibe, we present this sophisticated Snickers-in-a-scoop, with delicate chocolate shards and crunchy salted peanuts.

In the bowl of an ice cream maker, combine the base and caramel syrup and turn on the machine. Churn just until the mixture has the texture of soft serve, 30 to 40 minutes, depending on the machine.

While the ice cream is churning, pour an inch or so of water into a small saucepan and bring it to a simmer. In a heatproof bowl that can sit in the saucepan without touching the water, combine the chocolate and vegetable oil. Put the bowl over the saucepan, reduce the heat to low, and cook, stirring occasionally, until the chocolate is completely melted, about 2 minutes. Take the pan off the heat, but leave the bowl on the pan. The chocolate will stay warm until the ice cream is churned.

Quickly alternate spooning layers of the ice cream, a sprinkle of peanuts, and a generous spiral of melted chocolate into freezer-safe containers.

Freeze until firm, at least 6 hours or for up to 3 months. (See Freezing & Storage, page 15, for tips.)

SALTED CARAMEL APPLE SHERBET

Trade your stick for a cone and your caramel-coated apple for a tart, refreshing sherbet shot through with gooey caramel. Because the fairground classic can be a little sweet-on-sweet, we bump up the acidity with malic acid, and because bitter and tart flavors don't always vibe, we keep the caramel particularly light.

**MAKES ABOUT
2½ PINTS**

2   cups Sorbet/Sherbet Base (page 26)

1½ cups apple cider, preferably unfiltered

½   cup heavy cream

¼   teaspoon Diamond Crystal kosher salt

⅛   teaspoon malic acid, or 1 tablespoon lemon juice

¾   cup Perfect Ice Cream Caramel (page 119)

In a medium bowl, whisk together the sorbet base, apple cider, cream, salt, and malic acid. Pour the mixture into an ice cream maker and turn on the machine. Churn just until it has the texture of soft serve, 30 to 40 minutes, depending on the machine.

Quickly alternate spooning layers of the ice cream and drizzling on a generous spiral of caramel into freezer-safe containers.

Freeze until firm, at least 6 hours or for up to 3 months. (See Freezing & Storage, page 15, for tips.)

SECRET WEAPON Powdered acid extracts are an ice cream maker's secret weapon, allowing you to bump up acidity without adding liquid. The key is choosing the right kind from among the three main types:

CITRIC ACID: This offers the same sort of acidity you find in fresh citrus.

TARTARIC ACID: Also known by its street name, cream of tartar, this brings the distinctive tartness of grapes.

MALIC ACID: This matches the acidity of berries and apples (just the ticket in this Salted Caramel Apple Sherbet).

THE RIFFS

CARAMELIZED PINEAPPLE SHERBET

MAKES ABOUT
1½ PINTS

Inspired by the caramelized pineapple soda from Rachel's Ginger Beer in Seattle, this flavor will convince you (if you aren't already a fan) that caramel has magical properties. We combine bitter-edged scalded sugar with the fruit's tropical sweet-tartness—think pineapples charred on a grill—and the result eats like Juicy Fruit gum. Don't ask me why, just give it a try!

¾ cup ½-inch diced pineapple, canned or fresh

2 tablespoons light brown sugar

3 cups Vegan Coconut Base (page 27)

¼ cup Salted Caramel Syrup (page 159)

⅛ teaspoon malic acid, or 1 tablespoon lemon juice

Preheat the oven to 425°F. Line a sheet pan with parchment paper.

Toss the pineapple with the brown sugar to coat well and spread evenly on the lined pan. Toast in the oven until the pineapple at the edges of the pan starts to brown, about 12 minutes. Let cool.

In a blender, combine the coconut base, roasted pineapple (and any juices), and caramel syrup and blend until the pineapple is pureed to the texture of a chunky smoothie. Stir in the malic acid.

Pour the mixture into an ice cream maker and turn on the machine. Churn just until the sherbet has the texture of soft serve, 30 to 40 minutes, depending on the machine.

Transfer to freezer-safe containers and freeze until firm, at least 6 hours or for up to 3 months. (See Freezing & Storage, page 15, for tips.)

THE RIFFS

BANANAS FOSTER RUM CARAMEL

**MAKES ABOUT
1½ PINTS**

When Paul Blangé first caramelized bananas in butter, sugar, and rum at Brennan's Restaurant in New Orleans in 1951, he named it for a restaurant regular (Good evening, Mr. Foster) and served the result over vanilla ice cream. Our fully frozen homage features classic bananas Foster in a salted caramel-y drizzle swirled into freshly churned vanilla. We keep it vegan—coconut ice cream base, dairy-free butter—but you do you!

3   cups Vegan Coconut Base (page 27)

1   teaspoon pure vanilla extract

½   teaspoon Diamond Crystal kosher salt

1¼ cups Bananas Foster Caramel (below)

In a medium bowl, combine the ice cream base, ¼ cup water, the vanilla, salt, and ½ cup of the caramel and whisk until smooth.

Pour the mixture into an ice cream maker and turn on the machine. Churn just until the mixture has the texture of soft serve, 30 to 40 minutes, depending on the machine.

Alternate spooning layers of the ice cream and heaping spoonfuls of the remaining caramel in thick swirls into freezer-safe containers.

Freeze until firm, at least 6 hours or for up to 3 months. (See Freezing & Storage, page 15, for tips.)

BANANAS FOSTER CARAMEL

MAKES ABOUT 1¼ CUPS

1½ ripe bananas

4   tablespoons Earth Balance vegan butter

1   cup lightly packed light brown sugar

2   teaspoons molasses (not blackstrap)

1   teaspoon pure vanilla extract

¼   cup dark rum

1½ teaspoons ground cinnamon

¾   teaspoon Diamond Crystal kosher salt

In a small bowl, mash the bananas with a fork until smooth. Set aside.

In a small saucepan, melt the butter over medium heat. Add the brown sugar, molasses, vanilla, and rum. Attach a candy thermometer to the side of the pan. Cook, stirring frequently, until the mixture is melted and registers 240°F on the thermometer, about 6 minutes.

Stir in the banana mash, cinnamon, and salt and turn off the heat. Use a stick blender (the mixture is too thick for a stand blender) to puree the mixture.

Transfer the caramel to an airtight container and let cool before using it. The caramel keeps in the fridge for up to 2 weeks. Separation is totally normal; just make sure to stir the caramel well before using.

SALTED
SWEET
CREAM
WITH
HONEYCOMB
CANDY

MAKES ABOUT
2 PINTS

1¼ teaspoons flaky sea
     salt

3   cups 17% Butterfat
     Base (page 22)

¾   cup Honeycomb Candy
     pieces (recipe
     follows)

Honeycomb candy, also called hokey pokey and sponge candy, is a science fair experiment you can eat. When you add baking soda and cream of tartar to molten hot sugar, the whole thing bubbles up like the make-your-own volcanoes we all did when we were kids. When the mixture hardens, it becomes this incredible aerated slab of crunchy caramelized sugar, whose interior indeed resembles honeycomb. Mixed into ice cream—we salt the base to coax out the nuances of the dairy—the candy slurps up moisture as it freezes (like the meringues on page 137), so it develops the melty-outside/crunchy-inside texture that I can't get enough of.

In a small saucepan, combine the salt and ¼ cup water and cook over medium heat, stirring, just until the salt dissolves, about 3 minutes. (A microwave on low works, too!)

In the bowl of an ice cream maker, combine the ice cream base and salted water and turn on the machine. Churn just until the mixture has the texture of soft serve, 30 to 40 minutes, depending on the machine.

Use a spoon or flexible spatula to gently fold the honeycomb candy into the ice cream so it's well distributed.

Transfer to freezer-safe containers and freeze until firm, at least 6 hours or for up to 3 months. (See Freezing & Storage, page 15, for tips.)

• recipe continues •

HONEYCOMB CANDY

MAKES ABOUT 2 CUPS

2 teaspoons baking soda

½ teaspoon cream of tartar

¾ cup granulated sugar

¼ cup light corn syrup

1½ tablespoons unsalted butter

½ teaspoon fleur de sel

In a small bowl, combine the baking soda and cream of tartar and set aside. Line a sheet pan with parchment paper and spray it with cooking spray.

In a medium saucepan (too small, and the mixture will bubble over later), combine the sugar, corn syrup, and 2 tablespoons water and stir until all of the sugar looks wet. Cook over medium heat, stirring occasionally, until the mixture comes to a simmer, about 3 minutes.

Continue to cook, this time covered and *without* stirring, until the mixture has thickened slightly, about 3 minutes. Add the butter and fleur de sel, and use a heat-resistant spatula to stir well to completely melt the butter. Attach a candy thermometer to the side of the pan and continue to cook, stirring gently and constantly, until the syrup registers 315°F to 325°F on the thermometer, about 4 minutes.

Turn off the heat and quickly but thoroughly stir in the baking soda mixture (watch it all bubble!), doing your best to distribute the powders throughout the sticky mixture. Let the mixture bubble up and expand for 30 seconds, then immediately and quickly pour the mixture onto the sheet pan and use a butter knife or an offset spatula to spread it out to a relatively even layer that's just under ½ inch thick.

Let the candy sit, uncovered, until it has cooled to room temperature, about 2 hours. Use the back of a spoon to break it into irregular bite-size (about ½-inch) pieces.

Store in an airtight container at room temperature for up to 2 weeks.

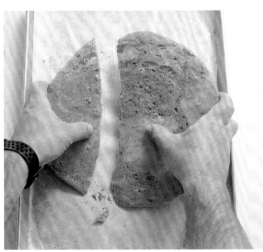

SALTED CHOCOLATE CUPCAKE

**MAKES ABOUT
2 PINTS**

3 cups 17% Butterfat Base (page 22)

¾ teaspoon Diamond Crystal kosher salt

3 Chocolate-Caramel Cupcakes (opposite)

Arguably one of Salt & Straw's most popular flavors ever, this recipe was created on a whim after our friends at Seattle's Cupcake Royale brought us a heap of day-old cupcakes. We took the bottoms and crumbled them into the ice cream after churning for a decadent texture that reminds me of when my grandma used to pour milk over chocolate cake, a dish we dubbed Midwestern Tres Leches. We kept the iced cupcake tops separate to create delicious pockets of frozen buttercream. Here we make our own moist, fudgy chocolate cupcakes with caramel icing for extra fun.

In a medium bowl, combine the ice cream base and salt and whisk until combined.

Pour the mixture into an ice cream maker and turn on the machine. Churn just until the ice cream has the texture of soft serve, 30 to 40 minutes, depending on the machine.

Meanwhile, cut the cupcakes in half to separate the tops from the bottoms. Chop the tops into approximately ½-inch chunks and crumble the bottoms to a gravelly texture.

When the ice cream is ready, gently fold in both chunks and crumbs of the cupcakes until well distributed. Transfer to freezer-safe containers.

Freeze until firm, at least 6 hours or for up to 3 months. (See Freezing & Storage, page 15, for tips.)

CHOCOLATE-CARAMEL CUPCAKES

MAKES 12 CUPCAKES

CUPCAKES

1¼ cups all-purpose flour

½   cup unsweetened cocoa powder

½   teaspoon Diamond Crystal kosher salt

⅛   teaspoon baking powder

¾   teaspoon baking soda

1¼ cups granulated sugar

⅓   cup vegetable oil

2   large eggs

¾   cup whole milk

FROSTING

10 tablespoons unsalted butter, at room temperature

½   teaspoon flaky sea salt

1¾ cups confectioners' sugar, sifted

⅓   cup Salted Caramel Syrup (page 159)

BAKE THE CUPCAKES

Preheat the oven to 325°F. Line a 12-cup muffin tin with cupcake liners and spray each with cooking spray.

Set a fine-mesh sieve over a medium bowl. Combine the flour, cocoa powder, kosher salt, baking powder, and baking soda in the sieve and sift everything into the bowl.

In a stand mixer fitted with the paddle, beat the granulated sugar and oil on medium speed until slightly fluffy, about 3 minutes. Reduce the speed to low, add the eggs, and mix until combined.

Turn off the stand mixer, add about half of the flour mixture, then mix on low speed until the ingredients are mostly combined, using a spatula to scrape the bottom and sides of the bowl. Add about half of the milk and continue mixing on low speed until mostly combined, another minute or so. Turn off the stand mixer, add the remaining flour mixture, then mix on low until mostly combined. Add the remaining milk and continue mixing on low until the batter is smooth, another 2 to 3 minutes.

Spoon the batter into the prepared muffin tin, filling each one about three-quarters of the way.

Bake until a table knife inserted in the center comes out clean, 20 to 25 minutes. Let the cupcakes cool completely.

MAKE THE FROSTING

In a stand mixer fitted with the paddle, combine the butter and flaky salt and mix on medium speed until the butter begins to turn a pale almost-white color, about 1 minute. Add the confectioners' sugar one-third at a time, mixing on medium-low for about 1 minute after each addition. Add the caramel syrup and mix on low until combined, about 2 minutes more.

Use a flexible spatula to transfer the frosting to a piping bag (or create a makeshift one using a resealable bag). Pipe a pretty swirl onto each cooled cupcake.

Refrigerate until chilled. Store in an airtight container in the fridge for up to 1 week.

BANANAS FOSTER
RUM CARAMEL

SALTED CHOCOLATE
CUPCAKE

CHOCOLATE CARAMEL
POTATO CHIP CUPCAKE

CHOCOLATE CARAMEL POTATO CHIP CUPCAKE

**MAKES ABOUT
2 ½ PINTS**

One of my favorite bites ever is the Highway to Heaven cupcake that Kir Jensen made at her late, great Portland dessert shop, The Sugar Cube. She made gorgeous chocolate cupcakes, filled them with salted caramel, topped them with ganache, and, get this, served them with a skyward-reaching crown of whole Ruffles chips drizzled with more caramel. We celebrate her creation in this gooey, mind-blowing scoop packed with ganache-glazed cake chunks, swirls of caramel, and chips coated with a delicious barrier made of chocolate to protect their salty crunch. Trust me, this one is worth the work it takes to make it.

3	cups 17% Butterfat Base (page 22)
½	cup Chocolate Mom (page 59)
1	tablespoon malt powder
¼	teaspoon Diamond Crystal kosher salt
¾	cup Chocolate-Covered Potato Chips (recipe follows)
¾	cup ½-inch pieces Ganache-Glazed Chocolate Cake (recipe follows)
¾	cup Perfect Ice Cream Caramel (page 119)

In a medium bowl, combine the ice cream base, Chocolate Mom, malt powder, and salt and whisk until smooth.

Pour the mixture into an ice cream maker and turn on the machine. Churn just until the ice cream has the texture of soft serve, 30 to 40 minutes, depending on the machine.

Use a spoon or flexible spatula to gently fold the potato chips and chocolate cake pieces into the ice cream so they're well distributed. Quickly alternate spooning layers of the ice cream and drizzling on a generous spiral of caramel into freezer-safe containers.

Freeze until firm, at least 6 hours or for up to 3 months. (See Freezing & Storage, page 15, for tips.)

• recipe continues •

CHOCOLATE-COVERED POTATO CHIPS

MAKES ABOUT 1 CUP

¾ cup chopped (chip-size pieces) good dark chocolate

¼ cup vegetable oil

1 cup Ruffles potato chips (gotta have those ridges)

Line a sheet pan with parchment paper and set aside.

Pour an inch or so of water into a small saucepan and bring it to a simmer. In a heatproof bowl that can sit in the saucepan without touching the water, combine the chocolate pieces and oil. Set the bowl on the pan and heat, stirring often, until fully melted.

Turn off the heat and use a spoon or flexible spatula to gently fold the potato chips into the chocolate until they're evenly coated.

Spread the chips on the lined sheet pan so that they're not touching each other. Chill, uncovered, in the fridge, until the chocolate hardens, about 30 minutes. (They keep in an airtight container in the freezer for up to 2 weeks.)

When ready to use, gently pull apart any clusters that may have formed.

GANACHE-GLAZED CHOCOLATE CAKE

MAKES ONE 9 × 13-INCH CAKE
(ABOUT 10 SERVINGS, PLUS
ENOUGH FOR 2½ PINTS
OF ICE CREAM)

CAKE

1 cup all-purpose flour

¼ cup plus 2 tablespoons
   Dutch-process or natural
   cocoa powder

½ teaspoon Diamond Crystal
   kosher salt

¾ teaspoon baking soda

¾ teaspoon baking powder

1 tablespoon finely ground
   (as for espresso) coffee
   beans

2 large eggs

1 cup plus 2 tablespoons
   granulated sugar

¼ cup vegetable oil

½ cup plus 2 tablespoons
   whole milk

GLAZE

5 tablespoons unsalted
   butter

1 tablespoon light corn
   syrup

½ shot freshly pulled
   espresso, or
   1 tablespoon extra-
   strong brewed coffee

¾ cup chopped (chip-size
   pieces) good dark
   chocolate

½ teaspoon flaky sea salt
   (I like Jacobsen Salt Co.)

BAKE THE CAKE

Preheat the oven to 325°F. Line a 9 × 13-inch baking sheet with parchment paper and spray it with cooking spray.

In a medium bowl, lightly whisk together the flour, cocoa powder, salt, baking soda, baking powder, and ground coffee to break up any clumps.

In a stand mixer fitted with the paddle, beat the eggs, sugar, and oil on medium speed until the eggs look lighter in color and slightly frothy, about 3 minutes.

Turn off the stand mixer, add about half of the flour mixture, then mix on low speed until the ingredients are mostly combined. Add about half of the milk and continue mixing on low until mostly combined, another minute. Turn off the stand mixer, add the remaining flour mixture, then mix on low until mostly combined. Add the remaining milk and continue mixing on low until the batter is smooth, another 2 to 3 minutes.

Pour the batter into the prepared baking dish and spread it out to make an even layer. Bake until a table knife inserted in the center comes out clean, 18 to 22 minutes.

Let the cake cool completely.

MAKE THE GLAZE

While the cake is cooling, in a small saucepan, combine the butter, corn syrup, and coffee and cook over medium-low heat until the butter melts completely and the mixture begins to bubble, about 3 minutes. Turn off the heat, add the chocolate pieces, and whisk immediately. Continue stirring until the chocolate is completely melted and the mixture has a glossy sheen. Stir in the flaky salt.

Pour the glaze over the cooled cake and use a spatula to spread it evenly over the entire surface. Cover with plastic wrap, transfer the baking dish to the fridge, and store until cold, about 4 hours. The cake can be stored in an airtight container in the fridge for up to 1 week (or 3 months in the freezer). When ready to use, cut the thawed cake into roughly ½-inch pieces and use while still cold. (Thaw completely before using.)

SALTED CARAMELIZED GRAPEFRUIT SHERBET

MAKES ABOUT
2 PINTS

¼ cup granulated sugar

2 tablespoons unsalted butter, at room temperature

1 tablespoon cornstarch

1 large grapefruit, halved

2 cups Sorbet/Sherbet Base (page 26)

1 cup whole milk

1 teaspoon pure vanilla extract

1 teaspoon flaky sea salt (I like Jacobsen Salt Co.)

In our salted caramel ultimate flavor, the sweet, salty, and bitter elements are at play. In this intensely flavorful sherbet, they return in particularly compelling combination. Grapefruit is front and center, with burnt sugar taking the grapefruitiness factor up to eleven and salt tempering the bitterness of both the citrus and the caramelized sugar so the fruit's flavor truly shines.

The addition of cornstarch is a little trick to help the sugar caramelize evenly (no burnt spots causing bitterness overload). The vanilla is a quiet player here, less a flavor you can taste than the reason the other flavors marry so well.

Preheat the broiler and position a rack in the top third of the oven (or ready a kitchen blowtorch).

In a small bowl, combine the sugar, butter, and cornstarch and stir to make a paste. Slather the mixture on the cut side of the grapefruit halves. Transfer them cut-side up to a small baking sheet.

Broil until the cut surfaces turn an even deep copper color and the sugar begins to smoke, about 3 minutes. Or, if using a blowtorch, hold it about 2 inches above the grapefruit and wave it in a circular motion until the tops are browned and charred in spots, about 2 minutes. Let cool slightly.

Use a spoon to scrape out all of the fruit, including the caramel topping, into a medium bowl, leaving the pith behind. Fish out any seeds. Add the sorbet base and use a stick blender (or transfer to a stand blender) to blend until fairly smooth. Blend in the milk and vanilla.

Pour the mixture into an ice cream maker and turn on the machine. Churn just until the sherbet has the texture of a pourable frozen smoothie, 25 to 35 minutes, depending on the machine.

Use a spoon or flexible spatula to fold the salt quickly but gently into the sherbet so it's well distributed. Transfer to freezer-safe containers and freeze until firm, at least 6 hours or for up to 3 months. (See Freezing & Storage, page 15, for tips.)

LEMONGRASS & FISH SAUCE CARAMEL

MAKES ABOUT
2½ PINTS

3   large stalks lemongrass

¼   cup gula jawa
    (Indonesian coconut palm
    sugar) or lightly packed
    dark brown sugar

3   cups 17% Butterfat Base
    (page 22)

½   teaspoons Diamond
    Crystal kosher salt

½   cup Fish Sauce Caramel
    (opposite)

This unlikely flavor came about when my friend Patrick Fleming of Portland's Boke Bowl challenged me to dessert-ify his incredible chicken wings. I immediately homed in on the caramel-y quality born when the sugars in the fish sauce marinade hit hot oil. To re-create it, I made caramel spiked with fish sauce and found that while the salt and umami were quite welcome, the result evoked the sea a bit more than I liked. A bold unrefined sugar, the kind common in Southeast Asian cooking, would've kept the fish sauce in check, but they're tricky to control at high heat. My solution: Stick to white sugar in the caramel and then use a gorgeous, intense Indonesian palm sugar called gula jawa for the scoop. A little lemongrass not only offers citrusy sweetness, but it also tones down the dairy flavor that might otherwise clash with the fish sauce.

Cut off and discard the bottom inch and top 5 or 6 inches from the lemongrass stalks. Remove and discard the outer layer and then thinly slice the remainder.

In a small saucepan, combine ¾ cup water and the gula jawa. Bring the mixture to a boil, stirring occasionally, then turn off the heat. Stir in the sliced lemongrass, cover the saucepan, and let steep at room temperature for 30 minutes.

Pour the mixture through a fine-mesh sieve into a container, pressing (and then discarding) the solids to extract as much liquid as possible. Use the lemongrass-sugar syrup right away or refrigerate in an airtight container for up to 2 weeks.

In the bowl of an ice cream maker, combine ½ cup of the lemongrass-sugar syrup, the ice cream base, and salt and turn on the machine. Churn just until the mixture has the texture of soft serve, 30 to 40 minutes, depending on the machine.

Quickly alternate spooning layers of the ice cream and a light drizzle of the fish sauce caramel into freezer-safe containers.

Freeze until firm, at least 6 hours or for up to 3 months. (See Freezing & Storage, page 15, for tips.)

FISH SAUCE CARAMEL

MAKES ABOUT 1 CUP

- 1 cup granulated sugar
- 2 tablespoons light corn syrup
- 2 teaspoons molasses (not blackstrap)
- ½ cup unsweetened coconut cream
- 2 tablespoons fish sauce (I like Three Crabs)
- 1 teaspoon soy sauce
- 1 tablespoon unsalted butter

In a medium saucepan, combine the sugar, corn syrup, molasses, and ¼ cup water and stir until all of the sugar looks wet. Cover, set the pan over medium-high heat, and cook, stirring occasionally, until the sugar has completely melted, about 3 minutes. Continue to cook, covered, but this time *without* stirring, until the mixture has thickened slightly, about 3 minutes. Uncover and continue cooking, without stirring but paying close attention, until the mixture turns a dark amber color, about 2 minutes more.

Immediately take the pan off the heat, stand back, and pour in the coconut cream in a thin steady stream (do not dump it in all at once!), stirring as you pour. It'll bubble furiously. Add the fish sauce and soy sauce and stir to combine.

Attach a candy thermometer to the side of the pan. Put the pan over medium-high heat again, and let the mixture simmer away, stirring occasionally, until it registers exactly 224°F on the thermometer, about 5 minutes.

Take the pan off the heat and add the butter, stirring slowly but constantly until the butter has completely melted. Let the caramel cool to room temperature before using.

This keeps in an airtight container in the fridge for up to 2 weeks. Separation is totally normal; just make sure to stir well before using.

Just a glimpse of that striking pale green, perched on a cone or peeking out of a cup, and you can practically taste it: the beguiling vegetal-sweet flavor of the pistachio. Perfected by the gelato makers of Sicily, home of the precious Bronte pistachios grown in the shadow of Mount Etna, the scoop made its way around the world. Including to Philadelphia, where in the mid-nineteenth century, or so it's said, a confectioner named James Wood Parkinson made the nuts into ice cream.

Pistachios, of course, aren't the only nut in the game. The West Coast is Pralines & Cream territory, and I'd say those golden scoops rival their green counterparts. But as you'll see, whether we're using the lush fat of almond butter or walnut oil to make especially velvety scoops or employing a sugary shield to incorporate the flavor *and* texture of macadamias and pecans, the classics are merely launch points. The possibilities for nuts are, well, *nuts*.

PISTACHIO GELATO 184

WALNUT OIL ICE CREAM 187

HAZELNUT PRALINES & CREAM 188

ALMOND BUTTER FLUFFERNUTTER 190

PECAN STICKY TOFFEE PUDDING 192

CARROT CAKE PECAN PRALINE 194

HONEY ALMOND ROCKY ROAD 198

CASHEW BRITTLE WITH PANDAN-
CILANTRO CARAMEL (V) 201

TOASTED MACADAMIA
WITH COCONUT JAM 204

OUR ULTIMATE

PISTACHIO GELATO

MAKES ABOUT
2 PINTS

3   cups Gelato Base
    (page 25)

¾   cup Pistachio Cream
    (opposite)

½   teaspoon Diamond
    Crystal kosher salt

¼   teaspoon green food
    coloring (optional)

½   teaspoon pistachio
    extract (optional)

Most makers buy the pistachio cream used for their ice cream—we're making our own. The first step is choosing the best unroasted (sold as "raw") Italian pistachios you can find. After all, the Italian nut is made for this moment, effectively grown to be blended into a paste—not chomped whole like, say, those from California—that has the particular bright-green flavor you expect from pistachio gelato. (Their skins come off more easily, too.) We stay away from roasted pistachios, because we've found that when nuts flavor the scoop itself rather than figure into the mix-ins, a dark, roasty quality can take over. Cold-pressed pistachio oil, which is easy to find, doubles down on that pure green flavor.

And the almonds in the recipe? Well, their harmonious effect on pistachios is one of the best-kept secrets in the industry. Pistachios, like strawberries, have a distinct yet subtle flavor when eaten by the handful. When you add pistachios to the necessary ice cream base, however, their flavor gets so quiet that it's hard to detect—even the distinctive color is faint. Most makers fill in the blanks with the bold extract of bitter almond and a dose of green food coloring. In fact, I've come across a few ice creams on the market with their titular nut missing entirely from the ingredients list.

In a medium bowl, combine the gelato base, pistachio cream, and salt and use a stick blender (or transfer to a stand blender) to blend until mostly smooth, 30 seconds to 1 minute. At this point, taste and, if wanted, stir in the food coloring and pistachio extract.

Pour the mixture into an ice cream maker and turn on the machine. Churn just until the mixture has the texture of soft serve, 30 to 40 minutes, depending on the machine.

Transfer to freezer-safe containers and freeze until firm, at least 6 hours or for up to 3 months. (See Freezing & Storage, page 15, for tips.)

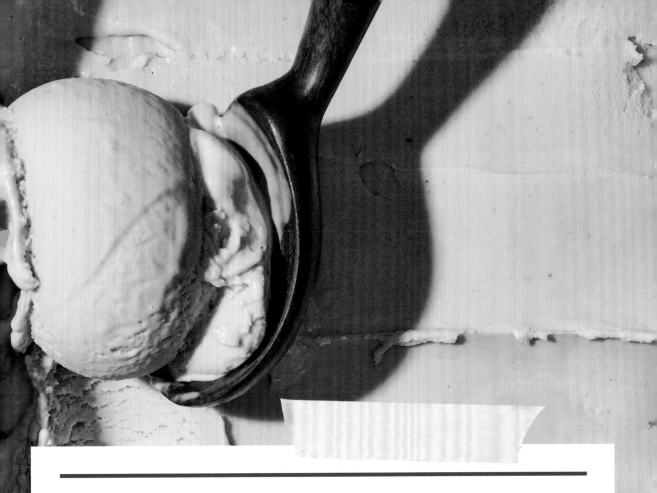

PISTACHIO CREAM

MAKES ABOUT 1½ CUPS

⅔   cup raw pistachios

⅓   cup raw Marcona almonds
    or other peeled almonds

1   cup confectioners' sugar

¼   teaspoon almond extract

¼   teaspoon Diamond Crystal
    kosher salt

2   tablespoons pistachio
    oil

½   cup heavy cream

Use your hands or a towel to rub the pistachios to loosen and remove their skins.

Bring a small saucepan of water to a simmer. Reduce the heat to maintain a gentle simmer, add the pistachios and almonds, and simmer until the nuts begin to soften and swell slightly, about 5 minutes. Drain well, discarding the water.

When the nuts are cool enough to handle, carefully remove any leftover skin on the pistachios. Once you've removed about 90 percent, you're good.

Transfer the pistachios and almonds to a food processor and pulse to a coarse paste. Add the confectioners' sugar, almond extract, and salt and pulse until the sugar is completely incorporated into the mixture, about 30 seconds. Add the pistachio oil, then blend until it creates a thick paste, about 2 minutes. Add the cream and process for another 3 to 4 minutes, until you get a light, creamy, smooth pistachio paste.

Store in the fridge in an airtight container for up to 3 weeks.

TRULY NUTS

Despite their popularity, most of us don't really know much about nuts, aside from the fact that peanuts and pine nuts aren't technically on the team. The former is a legume, as lovers of creamy, beanlike boiled peanuts can easily fathom, and the latter is an edible seed.

Ah, but guess what? Almonds, cashews, and pistachios—and this is truly nuts—aren't true nuts either! They're drupes—duh—or fruits with flesh surrounding a single seed, like peaches and plums. Ever see a cashew in the wild? They're so cool: Protruding from the reddish glossy-skinned cashew apple (which, by the way, contains no seeds and is therefore *not* a true fruit) is a chubby, little comma-shaped drupe. The drupe is harvested, dried, steamed, dried again, shelled to extract the kernel, and sometimes roasted.

Pistachios on the tree resemble flower buds, which ripen until the hulls (fleshy enough to make them drupes) separate from their hard inner shells as the seed inside grows larger. Some botanically minded folks are even reluctant to call walnuts and pecans nuts, choosing instead to split the difference with "nut-like drupes" or (my fave) "drupaceous nuts."

Congratulations, then, go to hazelnuts and chestnuts, which have a hard shell, no fleshy parts, and a single seed—making them legit nuts.

And congratulations go to us all as well. Because in a world where a fruit like cucumber is almost exclusively considered a vegetable and no one thinks about the fact that watermelon flesh is effectively fruit placenta, we get to enjoy them all, no matter what you call them.

KEEPING IT FRESH

Believe it or not, nuts aren't born in bulk bins at Whole Foods. As with spices, where nuts come from and how they grow tend to escape us. It's worth remembering that, unlike money, nuts do grow on trees, and so they're subject to the whims of terroir, producer priorities (e.g., productivity over flavor), and perishability. In other words, some nuts are better than others, and you want *those* nuts! Now, you can't often tell from packaging how long nuts have been

languishing on the store shelf, so your best bet is to look for nuts with provenance on the package (a start!) or, better yet, look for those from places known to do them right: hazelnuts from Oregon or Piedmont, pistachios from Iran or Sicily, and almonds from Northern California, Spain, or Sicily. Or, for you lucky West Coasters, buy from folks who grow and roast the nuts themselves, almost guaranteeing your nuts will be better than what's in those bulk bins.

WALNUT OIL
ICE CREAM

MAKES ABOUT
2 PINTS

3   cups 17% Butterfat
    Base (page 22)

3   tablespoons cold-
    pressed walnut oil

½   teaspoon Diamond
    Crystal kosher salt

There's walnut oil, and then there's gorgeous fresh cold-pressed walnut oil. Most of the stuff you see at grocery stores, because it's heavily processed, old, or both, tastes like only a phantom of the nut we know and love. But find yourself a top-notch product—our fave is from Fresh Vintage Farms, and they ship nationwide—and prepare to be floored as what you thought was a mild flavor explodes onto your palate.

Not only does walnut oil's addition to ice cream bring vivid flavor, but it also casts a spell on the scoop's texture that is pure magic (okay, fine, make that science). There's a limit to how much butterfat you can add to ice cream before it has an unpleasant, oily mouthfeel, but when you add nut oil—or olive oil, for that matter—the two different types of fat freeze together but don't technically merge. The result is a dreamily decadent texture that you could never get from butterfat alone.

In the bowl of an ice cream maker, combine the ice cream base, walnut oil, and salt and turn on the machine. Churn just until the mixture has the texture of soft serve, 30 to 40 minutes, depending on the machine.

Transfer to freezer-safe containers and freeze until firm, at least 6 hours or for up to 3 months. (See Freezing & Storage, page 15, for tips.)

HAZELNUT PRALINES & CREAM

MAKES ABOUT
2½ PINTS

Proper Louisiana-style praline—say it with us: PRAH-leen—is a marvel. Typically made with pecans, this confection features toasty nuts encased in a fudgy, caramel-y, melt-in-your-mouth mixture of cream, butter, and sugar. In ice cream, that coating serves as a delicious barrier, protecting the crunchy texture of the nuts while the candy edges melt just slightly to create enticing little pockets of extra sweetness. The nut is up to you, though hazelnuts, pecans, and almonds are particularly tasty.

3   cups 17% Butterfat Base (page 22)

¼   teaspoon Diamond Crystal kosher salt

1   cup ½-inch chunks Hazelnut Praline (below)

½   cup Perfect Ice Cream Caramel (page 119; optional)

In the bowl of an ice cream maker, combine the ice cream base and salt and turn on the machine. Churn just until the mixture has the texture of soft serve, 30 to 40 minutes, depending on the machine.

Use a spoon or flexible spatula to gently fold the praline into the ice cream so it's well distributed. Quickly alternate spooning layers of the ice cream and drizzling on thin swirls of the caramel (if using) into freezer-safe containers.

Freeze until firm, at least 6 hours or for up to 3 months. (See Freezing & Storage, page 15, for tips.)

HAZELNUT PRALINE

MAKES ABOUT 2⅓ CUPS
CANDIED NUTS

⅔   cup granulated sugar

⅓   cup lightly packed light brown sugar

3   tablespoons unsalted butter

¼   cup whole milk

2   cups unsalted roasted hazelnuts, roughly chopped

½   teaspoon pure vanilla extract

½   teaspoon Diamond Crystal kosher salt

Line a large baking sheet with parchment paper.

In a small saucepan, stir together the granulated sugar, brown sugar, butter, and milk. Attach a candy thermometer to the side of the pan. Set the pan over medium-high heat and cook, stirring occasionally, until the mixture registers 240°F on the thermometer. It's okay if it starts to crystallize.

Turn off the heat, add the hazelnuts, vanilla, and salt and stir until the nuts are evenly coated. Let the nuts sit in the pan for 5 minutes to cool slightly, then stir them one last time. At this point the sugar should start to seize and stick to the nuts like a thick paste resembling nut butter.

Spoon the nutty paste in half-dollar-size dollops onto the lined pan to cool completely. Transfer to an airtight container, breaking up clusters into about ½-inch chunks. Use immediately or store in an airtight container at room temperature for up to 2 weeks.

ALMOND BUTTER FLUFFER-NUTTER

**MAKES ABOUT
2½ PINTS**

Nut butter is another way to add a major infusion of flavor to ice cream. The key is not going overboard (too much can stiffen the ice cream). You want to add just enough to reap its incredible contributions to flavor and texture—big-time nuttiness and a velvety creaminess. Any pure almond butter works, but finding an especially roasty one pays off big time. Homemade marshmallow creme and bread—in this case, butter-toasted brioche that freezes to a toasty marshmallow texture itself— make this the finest of fluffernutters.

3	cups 17% Butterfat Base (page 22)
½	cup almond butter
½	teaspoon ground cinnamon
¼	teaspoon Diamond Crystal kosher salt
¾	cup Butter-Toasted Brioche Crumble (below)
1	cup marshmallow creme, store-bought or homemade (opposite)

In a medium bowl, combine ½ cup of the base and the almond butter and stir until well combined. Add the remaining 2½ cups base, the cinnamon, and salt and stir well.

Pour the mixture into an ice cream maker and turn on the machine. Churn just until the ice cream has the texture of soft serve, 30 to 40 minutes, depending on the machine.

Use a spoon or flexible spatula to gently fold the brioche crumble into the ice cream so it's well distributed. Quickly alternate spooning layers of the ice cream and generous dollops of marshmallow creme into freezer-safe containers.

Freeze until firm, at least 6 hours or for up to 3 months. (See Freezing & Storage, page 15, for tips.)

BUTTER-TOASTED BRIOCHE CRUMBLE

MAKES ABOUT 2¼ CUPS

6	tablespoons salted butter
3	thick slices brioche bread, torn into ½-inch pieces (about 2½ cups)

In a medium skillet, melt the butter over medium heat. When it begins to bubble, add the brioche in a single layer and cook, flipping once, until the bread turns dark amber on both sides and begins to crisp up, about 1 minute per side. Transfer to paper towels to drain. Let cool to room temperature. The crumble keeps in an airtight container at room temperature for up to 5 days.

MARSHMALLOW CREME

MAKES ABOUT 6 CUPS

3   large egg whites
    (without even a speck
    of yolk!)
½   teaspoon cream of tartar
⅔   cup light corn syrup
¼   cup granulated sugar

In a stand mixer fitted with the whisk, beat the egg whites on medium-high speed just until they look frothy. Add the cream of tartar and continue to beat until the whites reach soft peak stage, 2 to 3 minutes. Reduce the mixer speed to the lowest setting and let that run while you make the sugar syrup.

In a medium saucepan, mix the corn syrup, sugar, and ¼ cup water and attach a candy thermometer to the pan. Cook over medium-high heat, stirring constantly, until the syrup goes from cloudy to clear. Stop stirring and continue heating over medium-high until the syrup reaches 238°F.

Immediately remove the pan from the heat, increase the mixer speed to medium-low, and drizzle the hot sugar syrup into the mixer in a thin, steady stream, aiming for the hot sugar to hit only the egg whites and not the bowl.

Once the syrup is well incorporated, increase the speed to medium-high and beat until the mixture looks glossy and has cooled until it is warm to the touch, about 3 minutes.

Transfer the creme to a container and then use it immediately or cover and refrigerate for up to 1 week.

PECAN STICKY TOFFEE PUDDING

Ooey-gooey is a fantastic texture for ice cream mix-ins. And what's more ooey-gooey than toffee pudding—a lush, sticky date cake slathered with toffee sauce? Stirred into freshly churned ice cream, the dollops of pudding scream for a roasty, nutty counterpoint, and pecans step gallantly into the role.

MAKES ABOUT 2 PINTS

3   cups Rich Custard Base (page 24)

⅛   teaspoon ground cinnamon

¼   teaspoon Diamond Crystal kosher salt

¼   teaspoon pure vanilla extract

1½ cups Pecan Toffee Pudding (opposite)

In the bowl of an ice cream maker, combine the ice cream base, cinnamon, salt, and vanilla and turn on the machine. Churn just until the mixture has the texture of soft serve, 30 to 40 minutes depending on the machine.

Dollop tablespoon-size chunks of the pudding into the ice cream and gently fold to distribute the dollops without breaking them up too much. Transfer the ice cream to freezer-safe containers.

Freeze until firm, at least 6 hours or for up to 3 months. (See Freezing & Storage, page 15, for tips.)

PECAN TOFFEE PUDDING

MAKES ONE 8 × 8-INCH DISH
(10 SERVINGS, PLUS ENOUGH
FOR 2 PINTS OF ICE CREAM)

CAKE

- ½   cup all-purpose flour
- ⅓   cup lightly packed dark brown sugar
- ¼   cup pitted dates, roughly chopped
- 2   tablespoons unsalted butter
- 1   large egg
- ½   teaspoon baking soda
- ½   teaspoon pure vanilla extract
- ⅛   teaspoon Diamond Crystal kosher salt
- ¼   cup roughly chopped unsalted roasted pecans

SAUCE

- 1   cup heavy cream
- ⅓   cup lightly packed dark brown sugar
- 4   tablespoons (½ stick) unsalted butter
- ⅛   teaspoon Diamond Crystal kosher salt
- ¼   cup unsalted roasted pecans, roughly chopped

BAKE THE CAKE

Preheat the oven to 350°F. Spray an 8 × 8-inch baking dish with cooking spray.

In a food processor, combine the flour, brown sugar, dates, butter, egg, baking soda, vanilla, and salt and process to a smooth paste. Add the pecans and pulse until the nuts are in pieces no larger than ¼ inch.

Dump the mixture into the prepared baking dish and use a spoon to spread it evenly. Bake until the pudding is lightly browned on top and a knife inserted in the center comes out clean, 20 to 25 minutes.

Remove from the oven and let it hang out at room temperature while you make the sauce. Leave the oven on.

MAKE THE SAUCE

In a small saucepan, combine the cream, brown sugar, butter, and salt and bring to a boil over medium heat, stirring often. Constantly stir until the sauce thickens (you will start to see the bottom of the saucepan between stirs), about 1 minute. Remove from the heat and stir in the pecans.

Preheat the broiler and position a rack about 4 inches from the heat source.

Pour the sauce over the top of the cake and use a spoon to evenly spread the nuts over the top. Broil, keeping a close eye on it, just until the syrup no longer looks wet to the touch and the edges look crunchy, about 3 minutes. Don't let it start to give off smoke!

Let the pudding cool, then chill in the fridge. It keeps in an airtight container in the fridge for up to 1 week.

CARROT CAKE PECAN PRALINE

MAKES ABOUT 2½ PINTS

4   medium carrots, well scrubbed

3   cups 17% Butterfat Base (page 22)

1   teaspoon ground cinnamon

¼   teaspoon ground nutmeg

⅛   teaspoon ground cloves

½   teaspoon Diamond Crystal kosher salt

¾   cup ¼-inch pieces Carrot Cake (recipe follows)

½   cup Pecan Praline Crumble (page 197)

¾   cup Liquid Cheesecake (page 103)

We definitely go overboard with this one. But hot dang, is it delicious! We bake off a super-moist carrot cake. Then we candy pecans: Sweet and buttery, they're my carrot cake nut of choice, though walnuts work, too. We make what I like to call liquid cheesecake, which freezes to the creamy texture of freshly whipped icing. And finally, there's the ice cream itself—made with the juice of carrots that have been briefly charred on the outside. That way, you get that bright, refreshing quality of the raw veg as well as the moody complexity of the roasted.

Cut the carrots in half crosswise and carefully slice off the rounded sides to turn the carrots roughly into rectangular blocks (you need flat sides for pan-roasting).

Heat a heavy-bottomed skillet (preferably cast-iron) over high heat until it's nearly smoking. Using tongs, add the carrots to the skillet and cook, without moving them, until the bottoms begin to blacken, about 1 minute per side. Turn the carrots and repeat the process until every side of each carrot is seared; you want carrots that are blackened all over but still totally raw in the middle.

If you're using a juicer, pass each chunk of carrot through the machine. If you're using a blender, add the carrots and ¼ cup water to the bowl of the machine and blend until it reaches a smoothie texture. Strain the juice through a fine-mesh sieve, pressing (and then discarding) the solids. If making ahead, store the roasted carrot juice in an airtight container in the refrigerator for up to 3 days.

In the bowl of an ice cream maker, combine ¾ cup of the roasted carrot juice, the ice cream base, cinnamon, nutmeg, cloves, and salt and turn on the machine. Churn just until the mixture has the texture of soft serve, 30 to 40 minutes, depending on the machine.

Use a spoon or flexible spatula to gently fold the carrot cake pieces and pecan praline crumble into the ice cream so they're well distributed. Quickly alternate spooning layers of the ice cream and generous dollops of liquid cheesecake into freezer-safe containers.

Freeze until firm, at least 6 hours or for up to 3 months. (See Freezing & Storage, page 15, for tips.)

• recipe continues •

CARROT CAKE

MAKES ONE 8 × 8-INCH CAKE
(8 SERVINGS, PLUS ENOUGH
FOR 2 PINTS OF ICE CREAM)

2½ cups all-purpose flour

1   tablespoon unsweetened
    cocoa powder

2   teaspoons baking soda

2   teaspoons Diamond
    Crystal kosher salt

1   tablespoon ground
    cinnamon

½   teaspoon ground ginger

½   teaspoon ground cloves

2   cups granulated sugar

1½ cups vegetable oil

5   large eggs

2   tablespoons molasses
    (not blackstrap)

2   cups shredded carrots

½   cup canned crushed
    pineapple, drained

Preheat the oven to 350°F. Line an 8 × 8-inch baking dish with parchment paper and spray with cooking spray.

Use a fine-mesh sieve to sift together the flour, cocoa powder, baking soda, salt, cinnamon, ginger, and cloves. Set aside.

In a stand mixer fitted with the paddle, combine the sugar, oil, eggs, and molasses and mix on medium speed until the sugar has mostly dissolved, about 2 minutes. Stop the mixer, add the sifted flour mixture, and mix on low speed until just combined, about 30 seconds. Add the carrots and pineapple and mix until just combined, another 30 seconds.

Pour the batter into the prepared baking dish and spread it evenly. Bake until the cake is set in the center, about 45 minutes. (It's a very moist cake, so when it's set, a butter knife inserted in the center will still have some wet crumbs clinging to it.)

Let the cake cool completely, about 1 hour. Use immediately or cover and store in the refrigerator for up to 1 week. Cut the cake into ¼-inch pieces before using in the ice cream.

PECAN PRALINE CRUMBLE

MAKES A GENEROUS ½ CUP

⅓ cup roasted pecans, roughly chopped

¼ teaspoon Diamond Crystal kosher salt

¾ cup granulated sugar

Line a small baking sheet with parchment paper and coat the paper with cooking spray. Spread the pecans on the parchment in a crowded single layer and sprinkle the salt on top.

In a small saucepan, stir together the sugar and 1 tablespoon water until the sugar is hydrated. Attach a candy thermometer to the side of the pan and set over medium-high heat. Cook, stirring often, until the sugar begins to bubble, about 2 minutes. Stop stirring and continue to cook until the sugar cooks to 300°F (in order to get an accurate reading, tilt the pan so the mixture pools around the thermometer), another 3 to 5 minutes.

Immediately remove the pan from the heat and pour all of the sugar on top of the pecans. Allow the candy-coated pecans to cool to room temperature. Once cool, pop them into the food processor and pulse them to a gravelly texture, ⅛-inch to ¼-inch chunks. Store in an airtight container at room temperature until ready to use or for up to 2 weeks.

HONEY ALMOND ROCKY ROAD

**MAKES ABOUT
2½ PINTS**

3   cups 17% Butterfat
    Base (page 22)

½   cup Chocolate Mom
    (page 59)

¼   teaspoon Diamond
    Crystal kosher salt

¾   cup Caramelized
    Almonds (opposite)

1   cup Honey Marshmallow
    Creme (opposite)

This classic was invented around the time of the Great Depression and named, or so one story goes, in part for a nut-and-marshmallow-studded candy popular at the time and in part for the rocky road ahead. Well, times are still rocky, if you ask me, but ice cream is here to provide a little joy. The secret to this scoop? Honey. Honey coats the almonds, protecting their crunch and lending them its complex, floral sweetness, and in the homemade honey marshmallow creme, aerated egg whites capture more of honey's aromatic qualities. The backdrop might be chocolate, but honey and almonds—who have been best buds since the birth of Honey Nut Cheerios—are the stars.

In the bowl of an ice cream maker, combine the ice cream base, Chocolate Mom, and salt and turn on the machine. Churn just until the mixture has the texture of soft serve, 30 to 40 minutes, depending on the machine.

Use a spoon or flexible spatula to gently fold the caramelized almonds into the ice cream so they're well distributed. Quickly alternate spooning layers of the ice cream and generous dollops of the marshmallow creme into freezer-safe containers.

Freeze until firm, at least 6 hours or for up to 3 months. (See Freezing & Storage, page 15, for tips.)

CARAMELIZED ALMONDS

MAKES ABOUT 1 CUP

1   cup unsalted roasted almonds, coarsely chopped
1   tablespoon honey
2   tablespoons granulated sugar

Preheat the oven to 350°F. Line a sheet pan with parchment paper.

In a small bowl, toss the almonds and honey together until the almonds are evenly coated with honey. Add the sugar and toss together until the almonds are evenly coated with sugar.

Sprinkle the nuts evenly onto the prepared sheet pan and bake until the sugar begins to caramelize around the edges of the pan, about 8 minutes.

Let the nuts cool to room temperature, then break up any clumps. Use immediately or store in an airtight container at room temperature for up to 2 weeks.

HONEY MARSHMALLOW CREME

MAKES ABOUT 5 CUPS

3   large egg whites (without even a speck of yolk!)
½   teaspoon cream of tartar
⅔   cup honey
¼   cup granulated sugar
1   teaspoon Diamond Crystal kosher salt

In a stand mixer fitted with the whisk, beat the egg whites on medium-high speed just until they look frothy. Add the cream of tartar and continue to beat until the whites reach soft peak stage, about 4 minutes. Reduce the mixer speed to the lowest setting and let that run while you make the honey-sugar syrup.

In a small saucepan, combine the honey, sugar, and ¼ cup water and attach a candy thermometer to the side of the pan. Cook over medium-high heat, stirring constantly, until the syrup goes from cloudy to clear. Stop stirring and continue heating over medium-high until the syrup reaches 238°F. Immediately remove the pan from the heat. Increase the mixer speed to medium-low and drizzle the hot honey-sugar syrup into the mixer in a thin, steady stream, aiming for the hot sugar to only hit the egg whites and not the bowl.

Once the syrup is well incorporated, increase the mixer speed to medium-high and beat until the mixture looks glossy and has cooled until warm to the touch, about 6 minutes. Add the salt and beat just until the salt is well combined, about 1 minute. Transfer the marshmallow mixture to a container and use it immediately or cover and refrigerate for up to 1 week.

CASHEW BRITTLE WITH
PANDAN-CILANTRO CARAMEL

HONEY ALMOND ROCKY ROAD

CASHEW BRITTLE
WITH PANDAN-CILANTRO CARAMEL

MAKES ABOUT 2 PINTS

¼ cup unsweetened shredded coconut

¼ cup raw cashews

¼ cup lightly packed light brown sugar

3 cups Vegan Coconut Base (page 27)

1 teaspoon Diamond Crystal kosher salt

¾ cup pieces Thai Chile–Cashew Brittle (recipe follows)

⅓ cup diced sweetened dried pineapple

½ cup Pandan-Cilantro Caramel (page 203), remelted if needed (see Note)

NOTE · THE CARAMEL CAN CRYSTALLIZE PRETTY EASILY, BUT DON'T FRET. IF IT DOES, JUST MICROWAVE ON THE DEFROST SETTING UNTIL MELTED, THEN WHISK OR STICK-BLEND UNTIL SMOOTH.

When I collaborate with chefs on ice cream flavors, they typically share a few of their favorite ingredients or an idea to get my wheels turning. And then there's Gregory Gourdet, who got so into the project that he just straight-up went and made me an incredible scoop of ice cream. Now that I've gotten to know Gregory, once a rockstar of Portland's Asian food scene and now the foremost practitioner of Haitian cuisine in the country, this makes perfect sense. I first met him while participating in a walk-around event where different chefs served bites to a thousand or so guests. Like most of the chefs there, I made a single dish. Gregory made eight. What's more, he mentioned offhandedly that the day before he had run a marathon. That's Gregory. Whatever he does, he goes all in.

So it probably won't surprise you that this is the most difficult recipe in the book. Persevere—it's so worth it. If you can't quite bring yourself to make the sorta-caramel spiked with pandan leaves (their vanilla-y, coconut-y quality is remarkable), at least make what I think is the star of the show: the shards of chile-spiked cashew brittle. Because crunchy cashews swathed in buttery candy is ice cream gold.

Preheat the oven to 325°F. Line a large sheet pan with parchment paper.

In a small bowl, combine the coconut, cashews, and brown sugar and toss to coat. Spread the mixture in an even layer on the sheet pan. Roast until the coconut around the edges of the pan turns dark roasty brown and the coconut in the center of the pan is golden brown, about 8 minutes.

Transfer the toasted coconut and cashews to a blender. Add the ice cream base and salt and blend on high until smooth, about 2 minutes.

Pour the mixture into an ice cream maker and turn on the machine. Churn just until the mixture has the texture of soft serve, 30 to 40 minutes, depending on the machine.

Use a spoon or flexible spatula to gently fold the cashew brittle and dried pineapple into the ice cream so they're well distributed. Quickly alternate spooning layers of the ice cream and generous drizzles of the pandan-cilantro caramel into freezer-safe containers.

Freeze until firm, at least 6 hours or for up to 3 months. (See Freezing & Storage, page 15, for tips.)

• recipe continues •

THAI CHILE–CASHEW BRITTLE

MAKES ABOUT 3 CUPS

1   cup granulated sugar

½   cup light corn syrup

1   cup raw cashews, roughly chopped

2   tablespoons coconut oil, preferably virgin

½   teaspoon Diamond Crystal kosher salt

1   teaspoon baking soda

½   teaspoon Thai chile powder

Line a sheet pan with parchment paper.

In a medium saucepan, combine the sugar, corn syrup, and ¼ cup water and stir until all of the sugar looks wet. Set the pan over medium-high heat and cook, stirring occasionally, until the mixture comes to a simmer, about 3 minutes. Continue to cook, this time covered and *without* stirring, until the mixture has thickened slightly, about 3 minutes.

Stir in the cashews, coconut oil, and salt. Attach a candy thermometer to the side of the pan and continue to cook, gently and constantly stirring, until the mixture registers 320°F on the thermometer, 8 to 10 minutes.

Remove the pan from the heat and quickly but thoroughly stir in the baking soda and chile powder (watch it all bubble!), doing your best to distribute the powders throughout the sticky mixture. Immediately (like superquick!) pour the mixture onto the prepared sheet pan, and immediately use a table knife or metal spatula to spread it evenly so it's just under ¼ inch thick.

Let the brittle sit, uncovered, until it has cooled to room temperature, about 1 hour.

Use your hands to break the brittle into irregular bite-size (¼- to ½-inch) pieces. Store them in an airtight container in the freezer until you're ready to use them as a mix-in (or to simply eat them) or for up to 3 months. There's no need to thaw the pieces before using them to make the ice cream.

PANDAN-CILANTRO CARAMEL

MAKES ABOUT 1½ CUPS

4   pandan leaves, fresh or frozen

10 cilantro sprigs (leaves and stems)

1¼ cups granulated sugar

¾   cup light corn syrup

2   tablespoons coconut cream (I like Aroy-D in a carton)

In a narrow container (one you can use a stick blender in), combine the pandan, cilantro, and 1 cup water. Use a stick blender (or transfer to a stand blender) to blend until the pandan and cilantro leaves are mostly pureed, about 2 minutes.

Strain the mixture through a fine-mesh sieve set over a medium saucepan, pressing the puree with the back of a spoon (press hard!) to extract as much juice as you can. Discard whatever's left in the sieve.

Add the sugar, corn syrup, and coconut cream to the saucepan and stir until all of the sugar looks wet. Cover, set the pan over medium-high heat, and cook, stirring occasionally, until the sugar has completely melted, about 3 minutes. Continue to cook, covered but this time *without* stirring, until the mixture has thickened slightly, about 3 minutes. Uncover and attach a candy thermometer to the side of the pan. Continue cooking, without stirring but paying close attention, until the mixture registers 226° to 228°F on the thermometer, about 3 minutes.

Let the caramel cool to room temperature, then use it right away or transfer it to an airtight container and store at room temperature for up to 2 weeks. Separation and some crystallization is totally normal; if necessary, remelt and stir the caramel well before using (see Note, page 201).

TOASTED MACADAMIA
WITH
COCONUT JAM

**MAKES ABOUT
2 PINTS**

3   cups 17% Butterfat
    Base (page 22)

1   teaspoon Diamond
    Crystal kosher salt

1   teaspoon pure vanilla
    extract, preferably
    Tahitian

¾   cup Candied Macadamia
    Nuts (opposite)

¾   cup srikaya (coconut
    jam), store-bought or
    homemade (opposite)

Macadamia nuts are so underrated. When they're good, they practically melt on your tongue and have this subtle, buttery sweetness that reminds me of top-notch white chocolate. Buy the best you can find—not random nuts from the supermarket that were roasted goodness knows when but macadamias from, say, a Hawaiian company dedicated to careful growing and roasting. (The internet is your friend here.) Coconut jam, too, deserves way more love, at least outside of Malaysia and Indonesia, where the beloved custardy egg yolk–enriched condiment is slathered on toast. (I love the Hey Boo brand.) Together, these two unflashy but worthy mix-ins become a decadent and beguiling combo in a scoop.

In the bowl of an ice cream maker, combine the ice cream base, salt, and vanilla and turn on the machine. Churn just until the mixture has the texture of soft serve, 30 to 40 minutes, depending on the machine.

Gently fold in the candied macadamia nuts so they're well distributed. Quickly alternate spooning layers of the ice cream and generous drizzles of the coconut jam into freezer-safe containers.

Freeze until firm, at least 6 hours or for up to 3 months. (See Freezing & Storage, page 15, for tips.)

CANDIED MACADAMIA NUTS

MAKES ¾ CUP

¾ cup roasted macadamia nuts

2 tablespoons light corn syrup

2 tablespoons granulated sugar

Preheat the oven to 300°F. Line a small baking sheet with parchment paper.

In a medium bowl, combine the macadamia nuts and corn syrup and stir to coat evenly. Pour in the sugar and toss to coat evenly.

Spread the nuts on the sheet pan and bake, stirring halfway through, until the sugar coating is completely dry and looks powdery white, 10 to 12 minutes.

Let the nuts cool to room temperature. They keep in an airtight container in a cool, dark place for up to 1 month.

COCONUT JAM

MAKES ABOUT 1½ CUPS

4 large egg yolks

¾ cup unsweetened coconut cream (I like Aroy-D in a carton)

¼ cup granulated sugar

2 tablespoons light brown sugar

2 tablespoons light corn syrup

⅛ teaspoon Diamond Crystal kosher salt

In a small bowl, vigorously whisk the egg yolks until they get frothy and lighten in color, about 1 minute.

In a small saucepan, heat the coconut cream, granulated sugar, brown sugar, corn syrup, and salt over medium heat, stirring often, until it comes to a simmer, about 3 minutes. Turn off the heat.

While whisking, drizzle the hot liquid about ¼ cup at a time into the egg yolks. Transfer the liquid back to the saucepan and cook over medium-low heat, stirring constantly, until the mixture thickens enough to coat the back of a spoon, about 3 minutes.

Transfer to an airtight container and refrigerate until cold to the touch before using. It keeps in the fridge for up to 1 week.

We interrupt your regularly scheduled programming to bring to the stage a contemporary classic, a scoop devoted to the joys at the bottom of the cereal bowl.

The combo of cereal and ice cream has a special place in my heart. As a kid, I remember looking to the cereal box when I wanted to spruce up ice cream. My best work back then: microwaving Grape-Nuts with milk and sugar and crowning the porridge-y result with a giant scoop of vanilla. In the decades since, cereal has become a common (dare we say a classic) partner to ice cream, starting as a must-have topping during the frozen yogurt craze of the early 2000s. During the same era, chef Christina Tosi, owner of Milk Bar, invented the delightful Cereal Milk flavor while working in the kitchen at Momofuku in New York City.

Over the years, we've gone wild pairing cereal and ice cream, mixing in delights like marionberry cornflake cookies and our homemade riff on Reese's Puffs (which are cheekily tossed in pulverized real-deal Reese's Puffs). But one concoction in this vein has inspired a cultish following: Pots of Gold & Rainbows, featuring Lucky Charms. In 2013, we released it as a once-a-year flavor on a Friday, and by Monday every last pint was gone.

POTS OF GOLD & RAINBOWS 210

POTS OF GOLD & RAINBOWS

MAKES ABOUT
2 PINTS

1¼ cups Lucky Charms

3 cups 17% Butterfat Base (page 22)

1 teaspoon pure vanilla extract, preferably Tahitian

½ teaspoon clear (imitation) vanilla extract

½ teaspoon Diamond Crystal kosher salt

While the formula and method for this ice cream can be applied to literally any cereal (see Ten Cereal Riffs, page 212), this recipe with a cultish following features Lucky Charms, the hydrogen bomb in the post-World War II sugar race between Kellogg's, Post Cereals, and General Mills. We celebrate both components: the cereal and the marshmallows.

Over the past twelve years, we've tried many ways to extract maximum flavor from cereal. Early on we steeped and strained until the flavor went viral and the small amount of expensive dairy we lost during straining began to add up. Later, we employed stainless steel cider presses (seriously, we did this), which minimized the loss but created a huge mess. Finally, we settled upon the best method, which also happened to be the simplest: Pulverize the cereal, mix it into the ice cream base, then don't do a dang thing else but churn.

Not to say we don't get rather particular about this flavor: We have pro pastry chefs in our kitchen working for hours not to make marshmallows but to sort them. And you should sort yours, too. Put on a podcast and give in to the meditative, childlike fun of separating golden cereal from pink hearts, yellow moons, green clover leafs, and the rest.

From the time this flavor took off at our shops, I have once a year emailed General Mills, the company behind Lucky Charms, to ask if they'd consider selling us the marshmallows separately. And every year, I've received a polite no, though the home ice cream maker is finally in luck: They just started selling small quantities of Lucky Charms Just Magical Marshmallows.

Spend a few minutes sorting the marshmallows from the cereal pieces. Put the cereal pieces in a spice grinder and grind to a fine powder. If you're finicky like me, sift through a fine-mesh sieve and discard any larger pieces.

In the bowl of an ice cream maker, combine the ice cream base, both vanillas, the salt, and cereal dust and turn on the machine. Churn just until the mixture has the texture

of soft serve, 30 to 40 minutes, depending on the machine.

Use a spoon or flexible spatula to gently fold the reserved marshmallow bits into the ice cream so they're well distributed.

Transfer to freezer-safe containers and freeze until firm, at least 6 hours or for up to 3 months. (See Freezing & Storage, page 15, for tips.)

TEN CEREAL RIFFS

To underscore just how easy it is to turn your favorite cereal into ice cream, we're sharing ten flavors, each with a little twist to play it up and to get your brain juices flowing as you create your own scoops. For every 3 cups of 17% Butterfat Base (page 22), use ½ cup of your favorite cereal, ground to a fine powder in a spice grinder.

CORNFLAKES & BERRY JAM

This combination of ice cream base churned with ground cornflakes is perfect for your favorite mixed berry jam. Stir to loosen ½ cup of berry jam and alternate layers of ice cream and swirls of the jam in your containers.

HONEY NUT CHOCOLATE & PEANUT BUTTER

Ice cream base churned with about 1 tablespoon peanut butter and ground Honey Nut Cheerios is like a Reese's-lover's dream come true. For decadent shards of chocolate, give it the chocolate stracciatella treatment after churning (see Chocolate Chocolate Chip, page 58).

SPICY CINNAMON TOAST CRUNCH

Combining the ice cream base with a pinch of cayenne pepper and ground Cinnamon Toast Crunch before churning is an incredible way to amp up the cinnamon cereal flavor.

BOOZY GRAPE-NUTS

Add a generous splash of bourbon to your ice cream base along with ground Grape-Nuts to help bring out the natural malty flavor of the cereal.

CAP'N CRUNCH & BERRIES

Combine the ice cream base with ground Cap'n Crunch and churn. Stir in freeze-dried berries right after churning for the ultimate Crunch Berries vibe.

CHOCOLATE CHIP COOKIE CRISP

Before churning, mix together the ice cream base with 1 tablespoon malt powder, 1 teaspoon molasses, and Cookie Crisp dust. The malt and molasses are the perfect flavors to make the chocolate chip cookies explode with flavor.

RUM RAISIN BRAN

Combine the ice cream base with about 2 tablespoons black rum and ground Raisin Bran flakes. After churning, stir in ½ cup of the raisins from the box for a fun riff on Rum Raisin.

GOLDEN GRAHAMS S'MORES

Churn together the ice cream base with Golden Grahams dust. Stir in ¼ cup miniature marshmallows. As you pack the containers, stir in drizzles of chocolate stracciatella (see Chocolate Chocolate Chip, page 58) to get full-on s'mores galore.

SALTED REESE'S PUFFS

Churn together the ice cream base, ½ cup Chocolate Mom (page 59), and ground Reese's Puffs. Sprinkle in a little flaky salt as you pack the containers to get pleasantly salty pockets in your peanut butter chocolate ice cream.

CINNAMON CHEX HORCHATA LATTE

Churn together the ice cream base with ¼ cup of any of the three coffee syrups (see page 111) and ground Cinnamon Chex. The ice cream itself is delicately and wonderfully reminiscent of a classic horchata.

GREE

Green tea ice cream was a classic in Japan for decades before the flavor joined the Häagen-Dazs roster in 1996, a sure sign that a scoop had made it in America. And while my friends from the Northeast remember the scoop as an olive-green option offered alongside red bean ice cream at Japanese restaurants, I recall ordering matcha soft serve from the mall in Seattle as a kid and being blown away by the vivid green color and naturally sweet, grassy flavor.

By the time I'd turned from ice cream-loving kid into ice cream-making adult, I started to wonder why we scoop specialists stop at just one star in the vast galaxy of teas. Some teas, after all, are a natural fit with milk and sugar (hello, chai!), and even those typically taken pure—that is, simply steeped in hot water—offer incredible possibilities through some thoughtful and creative interventions. The challenge is part of the fun!

MATCHA MATCHA MAN 218

CHERRY BLOSSOM GELATO 221

BIG HIBISCICLE 222

TOASTED MILK SHERBET ASSAM
TEA CARAMEL 224

APRICOT MEADOW MARMALADE 226

CHOCOLATE EARL GREY & LEMON
SHORTBREAD 228

SMOKED BLACK TEA WITH BLACK
SESAME MARSHMALLOWS 231

JASMINE MILK TEA ALMOND
STRACCIATELLA 233

OUR ULTIMATE

MATCHA MATCHA MAN

MAKES ABOUT
2 PINTS

3   cups 17% Butterfat
    Base (page 22)

2   teaspoons matcha
    powder, preferably
    ceremonial grade

¼   teaspoon finely grated
    orange zest

½   cup freshly squeezed
    orange juice

¼   teaspoon pure vanilla
    extract

I owe much of my love and understanding of tea to one man: the late legend Steven Smith. I met him through my cousin and business partner Kim, who met Steven in the early '00s when they both worked for Starbucks. He headed up their tea division. He once told me about a creation he had always wanted to put on the Frappuccino menu but never did. With his blessing, I decided to take up the task at our shop, channeling both his virtuosity for pairing flavors and his namesake company's sky-scraping standards to make what he named Matcha Matcha Man.

Yes, the scoop features matcha (the powdered pricey-but-worth-it shade-grown green tea)—and not just any matcha, but one that is intensely flavored top-grade tea. That is, the best of the best that's typically reserved for the traditional Japanese tea ceremony, where it's made with hot water (~175°F is the accepted ideal temp) and frothed in a bowl with a special bamboo whisk. To matcha, Steven added a dose of . . . orange juice. The effect is hard to describe, so bear with me: Matcha has a glorious grassy, umami-rich flavor. It tastes very, well, green. That green can be bright and happy but also a bit moody and dark, more forest than meadow. Served properly, steamy and frothy in a ceramic bowl, those darker qualities are divine, but cold with dairy and sugar, we want that brightness to come through. That's where sunshine-y OJ comes in to say, Hey, matcha, brighten up! It's an incredible thing to behold. Steven's who'd-a-thunk-it trick, based on his masterful understanding of how flavors work, made him the tea maker extraordinaire and is also what makes this flavor special.

In a medium bowl, combine the ice cream base and matcha powder and mix with a stick blender (or in a stand blender on low). Let the base and matcha rest for about 5 minutes to allow the matcha to hydrate. Stir again, then add the orange zest, orange juice, and vanilla.

Pour the mixture into an ice cream maker and turn on the machine. Churn just until the mixture has the texture of soft serve, 30 to 40 minutes, depending on the machine.

Transfer to freezer-safe containers and freeze until firm, at least 6 hours or for up to 3 months. (See Freezing & Storage, page 15, for tips.)

TEA MAKERS

After my friend and tea mentor Steven Smith retired from Starbucks, he devoted his life to his passion project, Steven Smith Teamaker. Throwing caution to the wind, he decided to seek out the finest teas on earth and combine them to produce products like nothing the world had ever seen.

He wasn't a tea grower. Rather, he played a little-understood role in tea making, one that has long inspired me as an ice cream maker, though I could only hope to be as skilled as he was. To explain, I need to first step back and answer a question that seems simple but is very much not: What is tea, anyway?

Technically, tea is made from the leaves of *Camellia sinensis*, a plant native to East Asia that has been made into a beverage for more than four millennia. Yet the word "tea" has come to refer to virtually anything that you steep in water and drink—from flowers (chamomile, hibiscus) and herbs (mint, rooibos) to aromatics (lemongrass, ginger).

Proper tea, however, is its own vast universe. Those leaves of *Camellia sinensis* are responsible for countless teas. The flavor, fragrance, color, and body depend on so many factors.

- There's the variety and where it's grown, of course. But there's also the altitude at which it's grown (the harsh conditions of mountaintops mean lower yields and, often, more complex flavors).
- There's the season in which it's harvested.
- There's the way it's grown (for instance, farmers erect canopies to shade tea plants and slow photosynthesis in order to produce matcha).
- There's how it's processed after it's picked—applying heat to freshly picked leaves prevents oxidation and yields green tea, but controlling oxidation creates new flavors in black teas like oolongs and darker, intense teas like Assam.

These are the factors affecting the raw materials available to tea makers like Steven. To make his teas, he worked like a master vintner, but instead of blending Merlot and Malbec in vats, he might bring together aged pu'er and cocoa nibs in sachets.

Along with vintners, tea makers are one of the earliest examples of flavor artists. They have blended teas and herbs for the purposes of both medicine and pleasure for a good 2,500 years. The amazing part to me, as someone whose job it is to make flavors, is how long the appeal of some of tea creations have endured. Jasmine tea was born in the Song Dynasty, when some savant thought to scent good old *Camellia sinensis* with jasmine blossoms. Earl Grey, the bergamot-tinged black tea, was created in the 1820s—nine hundred years or so after jasmine tea, it should be said—and is one of the most iconic flavor profiles. Salted caramel, by contrast, is only sixty-odd years old.

Whether we'll all still be drinking Steven's Meadow tea (a sunny chamomile blend with a natural honeyed sweetness) or his Portland Breakfast (a smoky, earthy version of the bold English blend) when cars can fly and we have our first AI president remains to be seen. But I recommend trying them now if you haven't already: smithtea.com.

CHERRY BLOSSOM GELATO

MAKES ABOUT
2 PINTS

3   cups Gelato Base
     (page 25)

½   cup fresh raspberries

2   teaspoons sakura
     (cherry blossom)
     powder

½   teaspoon Diamond
     Crystal kosher salt

¼   teaspoon pure vanilla
     extract

⅛   teaspoon almond
     extract

In Japan, people not only bask in the beauty of the cherry trees in the spring, but they also enjoy the gorgeous pale pink blossoms steeped in a cup of tea and infused into ice cream. Called sakura in Japanese, cherry blossoms are a prized sign of winter's end and have a really special floral quality that we capture here in gelato. Gelato ensures that the subtle sakura isn't dominated by butterfat and that the flavor, which we bolster with raspberry and almond extract, stays on your palate longer than it would in a sherbet or sorbet.

In a medium bowl, whisk together the gelato base, raspberries, sakura powder, salt, vanilla, and almond extract. Use a stick blender (or transfer to a stand blender) to blend until smooth (don't worry about the seeds), about 1 minute.

Pour the mixture through a fine-mesh sieve into the ice cream maker and turn on the machine. Churn just until the mixture has the texture of soft serve, 30 to 40 minutes, depending on the machine.

Transfer to freezer-safe containers and freeze until firm, at least 6 hours or for up to 3 months. (See Freezing & Storage, page 15, for tips.)

BIG HIBISCICLE

**MAKES ABOUT
1½ PINTS**

8   sachets hibiscus tea

¼   cup lightly packed
     light brown sugar

1   whole star anise

½   cinnamon stick

½   cup boiling water

2   cups Sorbet/Sherbet
     Base (page 26)

½   cup heavy cream

½   cup whole milk

2   tablespoons fresh
     lemon juice

½   teaspoon pure vanilla
     extract

Hibiscus is one of my top picks for iced tea. The dried flower yields bracing cranberry juice–like tang and tannins that make it super refreshing. No wonder hibiscus tea is beloved around the world, from Mexico (hello, agua de Jamaica!) to Egypt (karkadé, good day!) to West Africa (hey, bissap!). Some renditions add complexity with warm, sweet spices, and so do we: The star anise and cinnamon coax out the darker, wine-y notes of hibiscus. A good dose of lemon juice plays up the invigorating tartness of the flower and lets the bright color come through.

Pure hibiscus tea or a hibiscus-forward herbal blend works great here, though our favorite is Big Hibiscus by Steven Smith Teamaker, which you can easily buy online.

In a small heatproof bowl, combine the tea, brown sugar, star anise, and cinnamon. Pour in the boiling water and let the mixture steep for 8 minutes. Discard the tea sachets, star anise, and cinnamon and let the tea cool to room temp.

In a medium bowl, combine the cooled tea mixture, the sorbet base, heavy cream, milk, lemon juice, and vanilla and use a stick blender or whisk to mix until well combined.

Pour the mixture into an ice cream maker and turn on the machine. Churn just until the sherbet has the texture of a pourable frozen smoothie, 25 to 35 minutes, depending on the machine.

Transfer to freezer-safe containers and freeze until firm, at least 6 hours or for up to 3 months. (See Freezing & Storage, page 15, for tips.)

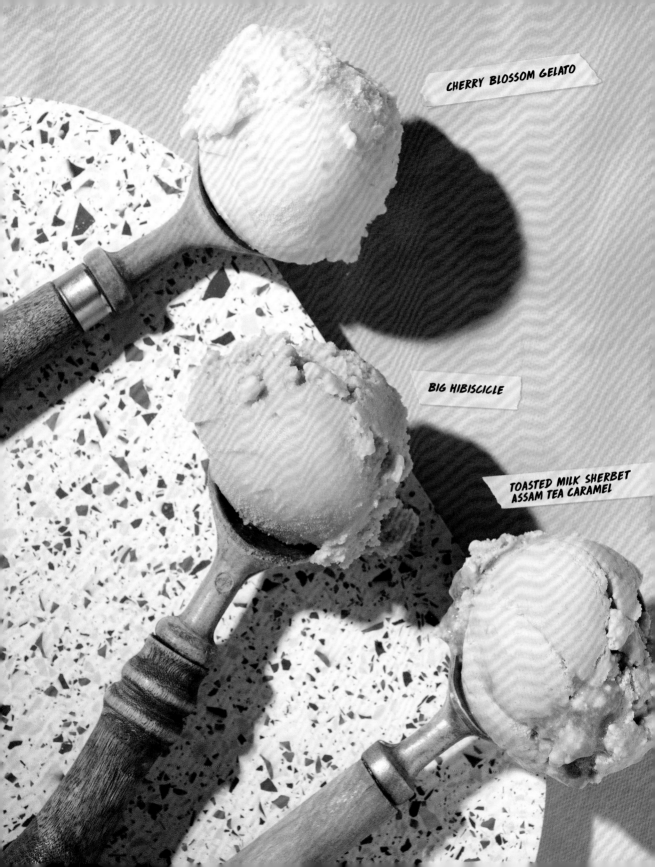

CHERRY BLOSSOM GELATO

BIG HIBISCICLE

TOASTED MILK SHERBET
ASSAM TEA CARAMEL

TOASTED MILK SHERBET ASSAM TEA CARAMEL

The dark complexity of caramel would overwhelm most teas, but not Assam. Whereas we'd turn delicate herbal teas into marmalade (see Meadow Marmalade, page 226), gooey caramel is a fabulous vehicle for the assertive, malty Indian black tea. To conjure a cup of milky Assam, we add swirls of that caramel to ice cream revved up with oven-toasted milk powder.

MAKES ABOUT 3 PINTS

- ¼ cup nonfat dry milk powder
- ½ cup hot water
- 3 cups Rich Custard Base (page 24)
- 1 teaspoon pure vanilla extract
- ⅛ teaspoon Diamond Crystal kosher salt
- ½ cup Caramel Assam Tea Swirls (opposite)

Preheat the oven to 325°F. Line a small baking sheet with parchment paper.

Spread the milk powder in an even layer on the lined pan. Toast in the oven, rotating the pan front to back and stirring every 3 minutes, until the milk powder turns an even dark amber color, 5 to 7 minutes.

In a medium bowl, combine the hot water and toasted milk powder and stir until well combined with no remaining clumps. Add the ice cream base, vanilla, and salt to the milk powder mixture and whisk to combine.

Pour the mixture into an ice cream maker and turn on the machine. Churn just until the ice cream has the texture of soft serve, 30 to 40 minutes, depending on the machine.

Meanwhile, put the Assam tea swirls in a warm place or gently warm in a small saucepan just until drizzle-able but not so warm that it'll melt the ice cream.

Alternate spooning layers of the sherbet and drizzling on about 1 teaspoon tea swirl into freezer-safe containers.

Freeze until firm, at least 6 hours or for up to 3 months. (See Freezing & Storage, page 15, for tips.)

CARAMEL ASSAM TEA SWIRLS

MAKES ABOUT 1¾ CUPS

2   cups heavy cream

4   sachets Assam black tea

1½   cups granulated sugar

¼   cup light corn syrup

2   tablespoons unsalted butter, cut into several pieces

½   teaspoon Diamond Crystal kosher salt

In a small saucepan, bring the heavy cream to a lazy simmer over medium heat, stirring occasionally. Turn off the heat, add the tea sachets so they're submerged, then cover the pan and steep for 10 minutes. Remove the tea sachets, gently squeezing any liquid back into the pan.

In a medium saucepan, combine the sugar, corn syrup, and ¼ cup water and stir until all of the sugar looks wet. Cover and set the pan over medium-high heat and cook, stirring occasionally, until the sugar has completely melted, about 5 minutes.

Continue to cook, covered but this time *without* stirring, until the mixture has thickened slightly, about 6 minutes.

Remove the lid and continue cooking, without stirring but paying close attention, until the mixture turns the color of maple syrup, about 6 minutes more.

Take the pan off the heat and immediately (with your face a safe distance from the pan!) begin *gradually* pouring in the cream mixture, stirring as you pour. Go very slowly at first, then work up to a nice steady stream.

Attach a candy thermometer to the side of the pan. Set the pan over medium-high heat again, bring to a simmer, and cook, stirring occasionally, until it registers about 230°F on the thermometer, 1 to 2 minutes. Take the pan off the heat, add the butter and salt, and stir to melt the butter. Let cool to room temperature.

This keeps in an airtight container in the fridge for up to 6 weeks. Separation is totally normal; just make sure to stir well before using.

APRICOT MEADOW MARMALADE

**MAKES
2 PINTS**

¾ cup roughly chopped (about ½ inch) fresh apricots

1 teaspoon pure vanilla extract

3 cups 17% Butterfat Base (page 22)

1 cup Meadow Marmalade (below)

One of my go-to strategies for celebrating tea in frozen form is making marmalade—that is, replacing the water you'd typically use to make the citrus jam for this ice cream with a concentrated cup of tea. The flavor is based on Meadow tea from Steven Smith Teamaker, a chamomile blend I drink several times daily. Set with a little pectin, the marmalade freezes to form fast-melting pockets of vivid, freshly steeped tea flavor in the ice cream, with a touch of dried apricot for added floral yum.

The marmalade formula works for any tea, so mix and match with your favorite leaves and a friendly citrus: Earl Grey and sour orange, oolong with key lime, and rooibos and grapefruit.

In a blender, combine the apricots, vanilla, and 1 cup of the ice cream base and blend until smooth.

Pour the mixture into an ice cream maker, add the remaining base, and turn on the machine. Churn just until the ice cream has the texture of soft serve, 30 to 40 minutes, depending on the machine.

Quickly alternate spooning layers of the ice cream and generous dollops of marmalade in thick swirls into freezer-safe containers.

Freeze until firm, at least 6 hours or for up to 3 months. (See Freezing & Storage, page 15, for tips.)

MEADOW MARMALADE

MAKES ABOUT 3 CUPS

6 sachets chamomile tea (preferably Meadow blend from Steven Smith Teamaker)

1 whole lemon

¼ cup fresh lemon juice

¼ cup powdered pectin

2 cups granulated sugar

In a small saucepan, bring 1 cup water to a boil and turn off the heat. Add the tea sachets, cover, and steep for 8 minutes.

Meanwhile, suprême the lemon by cutting off both ends of the lemon to expose the flesh. Stand the lemon on one end, then carve off the peel and pith following the curve of the fruit. Cut through both sides of each segment to remove it from the membranes and let the segments fall into a bowl.

Remove the sachets from the brewed tea, gently squeezing them to extract any remaining liquid. Stir in the lemon segments, lemon juice, and pectin. Set back over high heat and stir often until the tea comes back to a boil, about 1 minute. Add the sugar and cook, stirring constantly, just until it returns to a boil and the sugar is completely dissolved, about 2 minutes. Turn off the heat.

Let the marmalade cool to room temperature, then transfer it to an airtight container and refrigerate until completely chilled. It keeps for up to 2 months.

CHOCOLATE EARL GREY & LEMON SHORTBREAD

MAKES ABOUT 2 PINTS

Earl Grey tea was born in Britain in the early nineteenth century, when someone had the bright idea to hide the flaws of low-quality tea with oil of bergamot, a highly aromatic citrus. The flavor profile took off, and by now I'd wager we've all enjoyed a cup or one thousand. Those fragrant citrus oils go so well with chocolate, as does the strong black tea, its tannins matching those in the cacao. We also incorporate Earl Grey-infused shortbread: the buttery cookie is a classic partner for a steaming cuppa and a big hit in a frozen pint.

3   cups 17% Butterfat Base (page 22)

¼   cup Chocolate Mom (page 59)

2   sachets Earl Grey tea

1   teaspoon Diamond Crystal kosher salt

¾   cup small chunks Lemon Earl Grey Shortbread (opposite)

In a medium bowl, combine the ice cream base, Chocolate Mom, tea sachets, and salt and stir to mix in the chocolate syrup and completely hydrate the tea sachets. Transfer to the fridge and let steep for 45 minutes.

Remove the tea sachets, gently squeezing any liquid back into the bowl. Pour the mixture into an ice cream maker and turn on the machine. Churn just until the ice cream has the texture of soft serve, 30 to 40 minutes, depending on the machine.

Use a spoon or flexible spatula to gently fold the shortbread pieces into the ice cream so they're well distributed. Quickly transfer to freezer-safe containers and freeze until firm, at least 6 hours or for up to 3 months. (See Freezing & Storage, page 15, for tips.)

LEMON EARL GREY SHORTBREAD

MAKES ABOUT 12 COOKIES,
PLUS ENOUGH FOR
2 PINTS OF ICE CREAM

1   sachet Earl Grey tea

8   tablespoons (1 stick)
    unsalted butter, at room
    temperature

⅓   cup granulated sugar

¾   cup all-purpose flour

¼   cup cornstarch

½   teaspoon pure vanilla
    extract

½   teaspoon Diamond Crystal
    kosher salt

    Finely grated zest
    of 1 lemon

Preheat the oven to 325°F. Line a small baking sheet with parchment paper and spray it with cooking spray.

Open the tea sachet and dump out the tea leaves. Either very finely chop the leaves or finely grind in a mortar or a spice grinder.

In a stand mixer fitted with the paddle, cream the butter and sugar on medium-high speed until the butter takes on a lighter color, about 2 minutes. Stop the mixer and add the tea powder, flour, cornstarch, vanilla, salt, and lemon zest. Mix on medium-low speed until the mixture has just combined to form a slightly pebbly dough.

Dump the dough onto the lined pan, press it together, and use a rolling pin to roll it about ¼-inch thick. Bake until the shortbread is golden brown around the edges and dry to the touch in the center, about 15 minutes.

Let the shortbread cool to room temperature. Cut enough of the shortbread into small ¼- to ½-inch pieces to give you ¾ cup, then cut the remaining shortbread into cookie-size pieces. Use the ¾ cup chopped shortbread immediately for the ice cream or store in the freezer for up to 2 months. Cover and store the rest for up to 1 week.

SMOKED BLACK TEA
WITH BLACK SESAME MARSHMALLOWS

**MAKES ABOUT
3 PINTS**

½ cup boiling water

¼ cup granulated sugar

2 sachets lapsang souchong tea

1 sachet Earl Grey tea

3 cups 17% Butterfat Base (page 22)

½ teaspoon Diamond Crystal kosher salt

¼ teaspoon finely grated lemon zest

1 cup Black Sesame Marshmallows (recipe follows)

Grown in the mountains of China's Fujian province, lapsang souchong was likely the first black tea ever served. (Until sometime in the seventeenth century, tea was drunk green—*before* the leaves oxidized.) To assist in the drying process, farmers made fires of pinewood, and its smoke infused the leaves, so each cup has the incredible fragrance of a wood fire. It's a thrill in a creamy scoop—though we steep it in water, not cream, which would grab on to a little too much of the tannins and smoke. Black sesame marshmallows deliver some welcome nuttiness and a cold black color that calls to mind a cup of that deep, dark tea.

In a coffee mug, combine the boiling water, sugar, and all 3 tea sachets and stir. Set a timer and let steep for 8 minutes. Remove the tea sachets, gently squeezing any liquid back into the mug.

In the bowl of an ice cream maker, combine the tea, ice cream base, salt, and lemon zest and turn on the machine. Churn just until the mixture has the texture of soft serve, 30 to 40 minutes, depending on the machine.

Use a spoon or flexible spatula to gently fold the marshmallows into the ice cream so they're well distributed. Transfer to freezer-safe containers and freeze until firm, at least 6 hours or for up to 3 months. (See Freezing & Storage, page 15, for tips.)

• recipe continues •

BLACK SESAME MARSHMALLOWS

MAKES ABOUT 5 CUPS

½ cup black sesame
    seeds, preferably
    Korean

8   tablespoons
    confectioners' sugar,
    divided, plus more
    for coating

2   (¼-ounce) envelopes
    unflavored powdered
    gelatin (5 teaspoons)

¼ cup cold water

1   cup granulated sugar

⅓ cup light corn syrup

Preheat the oven to 325°F. Line a 9 × 13-inch baking sheet with parchment paper.

Spread the sesame seeds on the lined baking sheet in an even layer. Toast in the oven until the seeds look shiny as their oil starts to surface, about 6 minutes. Let the seeds cool slightly.

Combine the seeds and 1 tablespoon of the confectioners' sugar in a spice grinder and grind to a fine powder.

Spray the parchment (still on the baking sheet) with cooking spray, making sure to get the corners and edges. Sprinkle the remaining 7 tablespoons confectioners' sugar over the pan, rotating it to get the sugar to evenly coat the bottom, edges, and corners. Dump out and discard the excess sugar.

In a stand mixer bowl, sprinkle the gelatin over the cold water and use a hand whisk to gently stir to make sure it's all wet. Snap the whisk attachment onto the mixer. Let sit while you prepare the sugar syrup.

In a small saucepan, combine the granulated sugar and corn syrup and bring to a boil over medium-high heat, stirring occasionally with a heatproof flexible spatula, about 4 minutes. Attach a candy thermometer to the pan and continue to cook, now *without* stirring, until it registers 240°F.

Immediately remove the saucepan from the heat, turn the stand mixer to medium-low, and drizzle the hot sugar syrup in a thin, steady stream directly into the liquid (not the sides of the bowl). Increase the speed to medium-high and beat until the mixture looks glossy and has cooled until warm to the touch, about 4 minutes. Add the sesame seed powder and beat just until well combined, about 30 seconds more.

Scrape the mixture onto the prepared baking sheet, spread evenly, and let the marshmallow set at room temperature for 2 hours.

Once set, slide the parchment with the big marshmallow onto a cutting board, slice into ½-inch cubes, and toss generously with more confectioners' sugar to keep the sticky cut sides from sticking together.

The marshmallows keep in an airtight container in the refrigerator for up to 3 months.

JASMINE MILK TEA ALMOND STRAC- CIATELLA

**MAKES ABOUT
2½ PINTS**

½ cup heavy cream

¼ cup granulated sugar

½ teaspoon Diamond Crystal kosher salt

6 sachets jasmine green tea

3 cups 17% Butterfat Base (page 22)

¾ cup chopped (chip-size pieces) good dark chocolate

2 teaspoons vegetable oil

¼ cup blanched almonds, preferably Marcona, chopped into ⅛- to ¼-inch pieces

Green tea doesn't just crop up smelling of jasmine—to make the good stuff, master tea makers choose the sweetest tea leaves and toss them in great heaps with fresh jasmine flowers, harvested in the morning before they blossom. By controlling the temperature, the tea makers encourage the flowers to open so the tea absorbs their perfume. We use top-tier sachets and steep them in a mixture of water and cream (the fat pulls out even more of the tea's flavor). Chocolatiers often infuse floral, perfume-y jasmine into their confections, so I figured I'd add really nice melted dark chocolate, stracciatella-style, to my jasmine-flavored scoop, plus slivered almonds for texture.

In a small saucepan, combine the heavy cream, ¼ cup water, the sugar, and salt and bring to a lazy simmer over medium heat. Turn off the heat, add the tea sachets so they're submerged, then cover the saucepan and let steep for 12 minutes. Remove the tea sachets, gently squeezing any liquid back into the pan. Cool the steeped cream until it's at least cool to the touch before moving on to churning.

In the bowl of an ice cream maker, combine the jasmine-cream mixture and ice cream base and turn on the machine. Churn just until the ice cream has the texture of soft serve, 30 to 40 minutes, depending on the machine.

While the ice cream is churning, pour an inch or so of water into a small saucepan and bring it to a simmer. In a heatproof bowl that can sit in the saucepan without touching the water, combine the chocolate and vegetable oil. Put the bowl over the saucepan, reduce the heat to low, and cook, stirring occasionally, until the chocolate is completely melted, about 2 minutes. Take the pan off the heat and stir in the almonds; leave the bowl on the pan. The chocolate will stay warm until the ice cream is churned.

Quickly alternate spooning layers of the ice cream and drizzling on generous spirals of melted chocolate into freezer-safe containers. Once the containers are full, use a spoon to lightly stir the ice cream to break up any large chunks of chocolate.

Freeze until firm, at least 6 hours or for up to 3 months. (See Freezing & Storage, page 15, for tips.)

Alcohol in sweets in general—and in ice cream in particular—has a long, spirited history that we can trace back centuries before the rum raisin craze of the '80s and '90s. Yet if nowadays ordering vanilla says boring (which it turns out is rather ironic—see page 30), then ordering rum raisin says grandpa.

Or does it? Turns out, when you choose top-shelf spirits and use them with care and intention, boozy ice creams are anything but stodgy. Our extra-decadent rum raisin, for instance, will thrill both Pop Pop and his adult grandkids, who came of age in the era of the craft cocktail. In this chapter, we play with alcohol's antifreezing properties and employ its special ability to hold and transmit flavor (no wonder it's the base of vanilla extract), with cheers to a few of our favorite cocktails, captured in frozen form.

RUM RAISIN CUSTARD 238

ROSÉ FROZÉ (V) 242

FERNET & MAPLE 243

RAW RHUBARB & CAMPARI
SORBET (V) 245

AMARETTO SOUR SHERBET 246

KALIMOTXO CREAM SHERBET 247

CHAMPAGNE SORBET (V) 248

RUM RAISIN CUSTARD

MAKES ABOUT
2½ PINTS

3   cups Rich Custard Base
    (page 24)
½   cup Rum Raisin Syrup
    (recipe follows)
    Candied Rum Raisins
    (recipe follows)

To quote a representative Reddit post on this chapter's hero flavor: "I think all of the rum raisin fans are mostly dead at this point." Harsh! Well, not this one. Yet as much as I love the flavor, however uncool, I'll concede that it deserves, if not a makeover, then at least an update. So we skip the well liquor typically dumped into the standard-issue rum raisin and instead choose a nice dark rum that can stand up to the raisin's dried-fruit intensity, the kind of rum distilled from molasses and then aged in barrels so it develops notes like caramel or chocolate. We let the raisins slurp up the spirit, letting them take on its complex flavors as well as its antifreezing properties, so instead of rock-hard fruit nubs you get plump, juicy explosions of sweet boozy flavor. Then we go a step further, giving the raisins a light crystallized sugar coating to create yet another layer of fun. At home, I recommend using super-flavorful raisin varieties like Autumn Royal, Sultanina, or Málaga. After all, just as coffee and chocolate aren't one thing but many, so it goes with dried grapes.

The vehicle for these beauties is obvious: gorgeous, extra-rich custard. Because just think about all the great best boozy desserts—from tiramisu to baba au rhum, Grand Marnier soufflé to flan—they're all sumptuous from egg. The yolks in this scoop give it body and, as devotees of piña coladas and eggnog know well, rum loooooves body.

In the bowl of an ice cream maker, combine the ice cream base and rum raisin syrup and turn on the machine. Churn just until the mixture has the texture of soft serve, 30 to 40 minutes, depending on the machine.

Use a spoon or flexible spatula to gently fold the candied raisins into the ice cream so they're well distributed. Transfer the ice cream to freezer-safe containers and freeze until firm, at least 6 hours or for up to 3 months. (See Freezing & Storage, page 15, for tips.)

CANDIED RUM RAISINS & RUM RAISIN SYRUP

MAKES ABOUT ½ CUP RAISINS
AND ½ CUP SYRUP

- ½ cup raisins
- ½ cup packed light brown sugar
- ¼ cup dark rum
- ¼ cup hot water

In a small bowl, stir together the raisins, ¼ cup of the brown sugar, the rum, and hot water. Let the raisins soak until they've plumped up, at least 4 hours at room temperature or overnight in the fridge.

Preheat the oven to 325°F. Line a small baking sheet with parchment paper.

Reserving the liquid, drain the raisins. In a small bowl, toss the drained raisins with the remaining ¼ cup brown sugar to coat evenly. Spread on the baking sheet in a single layer.

Bake until the raisins develop an opaque, crunchy sugar shell, 6 to 8 minutes, stirring and rotating the pan front to back halfway through.

Let the raisins cool completely. The candied raisins and syrup will keep in separate airtight containers in the fridge for up to 1 week.

THANK YOU, SICILY!

The origins of rum raisin are a window into the history and evolution of ice cream. Because before rum raisin, there was the Sicilian invention called Málaga gelato.

Sicily is the birthplace of ice cream as we know it, but the frozen treat was not created overnight. Its slow evolution began with the arrival of the Arabs in the eighth century. They brought the treat known as sharbat, created in ancient Persia, made from fruit syrups poured over snow.

Well, there was plenty of snow on Mount Etna (so much, in fact, that it became a major export), and locals became accustomed to the joy of cold treats, a novelty centuries before refrigeration. The years passed and technology proceeded apace until one fine day—some say in the mid-seventeenth century—one could use ice to create more ice. You'd just mix some really cold water with good old sodium chloride. The salt lowers the freezing point of water, creating a frigid liquid that can freeze a tub of sweetened cream via conduction.

The advent created, as you might expect, an explosion in the popularity of icy treats. And while this part is conjecture, I bet that solving the whole freezing problem freed up the creativity of early ice cream makers to do things like, oh, I don't know, soak Málaga raisins (especially sweet and meaty Spanish sun-dried raisins made from moscatel grapes) in a local fortified wine called Marsala, then stir the plump, juicy result into vanilla gelato. This became one of the most popular flavors of the time, an old dessert trick (immersing dried fruits in alcohol) applied to a new dessert. Later, as rum took off around the world, the spirit took over for Marsala in many scoops.

BYE-BYE, BOOZE. HELLO, ICE CREAM.

The combo of booze and ice cream may sound a bit odd nowadays, but they have long been connected—from the freezing-cold sweet drink made with cream, eggs, and wine served in Catherine de' Medici's royal court to zabaglione gelato, the classic flavor dosed with Marsala, to the huge boom in ice cream's popularity in America during Prohibition. It turns out, when people could no longer have one intoxicating vice, they indulged in another.

Ice cream consumption in America soared with beer companies turning into ice cream production centers. Yuengling opened a dairy. Anheuser-Busch launched trucks selling 5-cent cups and 10-cent "bricks." An explosion of creativity led to the merging of candy bar and ice cream, giving us the Good Humor bar and the Eskimo Pie (originally, and superiorly, named the I-Scream Bar).

Drugstores even spiked the treat with bourbon, exploiting a booze-as-medicine loophole. And malt shops, aka soda fountains, aka ice cream parlors, took over for bars as the cool place to hang out. The boom went bust after the repeal of Prohibition and the beginning of the Great Depression, but the love it spawned? Never faded.

[VEGAN]

ROSÉ FROZÉ

**MAKES ABOUT
2½ PINTS**

1   cup raspberries

½   cup your favorite
    rosé or any blush
    wine

1   tablespoon fresh
    lime juice

2   cups Sorbet/Sherbet
    Base (page 26)

In the summer of 2019, I'd swear every bar in Portland, Oregon, was serving frosé, a slushy take on the pink wine. While many high-volume wine makers cheat by mixing white wine with a touch of red, true rosé is made from red grapes that spend only a short time macerating with their skins, picking up a little color and some nice complexity to boot. Chilled, it's heaven in summertime, and so is this incredibly refreshing scoop made with a generous splash of rosé (just enough to add flavor without affecting the freezing) as well as raspberries to bolster its tart, winy flavor. When I pop open a pint at home, I almost always add a little swirl of raspberry jam and whipped cream to my scoop.

In a blender, combine the raspberries, 1 cup water, the rosé, and lime juice and blend until mostly smooth (don't worry about the seeds), about 2 minutes.

Pour through a fine-mesh sieve into a medium bowl, pressing (then discarding) the solids to extract as much juice as possible. Stir in the sorbet base.

Pour the mixture into an ice cream maker and turn on the machine. Churn just until the sorbet has the texture of a pourable frozen smoothie, 25 to 35 minutes, depending on the machine.

Transfer to freezer-safe containers and freeze until firm, at least 6 hours or for up to 3 months. (See Freezing & Storage, page 15, for tips.)

FERNET & MAPLE

**MAKES ABOUT
2 PINTS**

1½ cups Sorbet/Sherbet
     Base (page 26)

1½ cups whole milk

½   cup Fernet-Branca

¼   cup dark maple syrup

Sure, amaro ice cream sounds a little odd at first. But if you think about it, the gloriously sweet-bitter Italian digestif isn't so different from intense, alcohol-based flavor extracts like vanilla and mint, or root beers, which offer similar notes of sassafras, cherry bark, and licorice. If anything, amaro, a liquor steeped with various herbs and barks (sometimes hundreds in a single amaro!), is even more complex. This recipe will work with practically any bottle you like. Fernet is both one of the more polarizing and most popular amaros, which is why I chose it here: In the scoop, its menthol-y, bitter flavor becomes more nuanced. One thing's for sure: You've never had a scoop like this one.

In a medium bowl, whisk together the sorbet base, milk, Fernet, and maple syrup until well combined.

Pour the mixture into an ice cream maker and turn on the machine. Churn just until the sherbet has the texture of soft serve, 30 to 40 minutes, depending on the machine.

Transfer to freezer-safe containers and freeze until firm, at least 6 hours or for up to 3 months. (See Freezing & Storage, page 15, for tips.)

RAW RHUBARB &
CAMPARI SORBET

KALIMOTXO
CREAM SHERBET

AMARETTO SOUR
SHERBET

RAW RHUBARB & CAMPARI SORBET

MAKES ABOUT 1½ PINTS

1 cup ¼-inch-thick slices rhubarb (about 4 medium stalks)

½ cup Campari

½ cup warm water

¼ cup granulated sugar

2 cups Sorbet/Sherbet Base (page 26)

¾ cup sparkling water

¼ cup freshly squeezed orange juice

Without dairy to shush flavor, sorbets are a great way to feature loud fruits and vegetables. So one day I decided to make a sorbet not with the typical strawberry or mango but with the wildly underappreciated flavor of raw rhubarb. Vegetal, strikingly bitter, and tart, rhubarb almost literally dances on your tongue—or at least, with its tingly acidity from the stalk's natural oxalic acid, you certainly feel the footsteps. (The leaves, though, are toxic.) We pair it with Campari, the Italian liqueur made with rhubarb and orange that itself is bitter enough to grab the back of your cheeks. Somehow the bitter-on-bitter works wonders, especially with the sugar necessary to achieve the dense web of tiny ice crystals known as sorbet and orange juice to play up the sweeter elements of the Campari.

In a blender, combine the rhubarb, Campari, water, and sugar. Let it hang out for 15 minutes to let the rhubarb soften, then blend until smooth.

Strain through a fine-mesh sieve into a medium bowl. Add the sorbet base, sparkling water, and orange juice and whisk until well combined.

Pour the mixture into the ice cream maker and turn on the machine. Churn just until the sorbet has the texture of a pourable frozen smoothie, 25 to 35 minutes, depending on the machine.

Transfer to freezer-safe containers and freeze until firm, at least 6 hours or for up to 3 months. (See Freezing & Storage, page 15, for tips.)

AMARETTO SOUR SHERBET

MAKES ABOUT
2 PINTS

1½ cups Sorbet/Sherbet
    Base (page 26)

1   cup whole milk

½   cup heavy cream

⅓   cup amaretto

2   tablespoons finely
    grated lemon zest
    (grated on a
    Microplane)

¼   cup fresh lemon juice

1   cup Honey Marshmallow
    Creme (page 199) or
    store-bought
    Marshmallow Fluff

Until I met Jeffrey Morgenthaler, a Portland mixologist and one of the best of his generation, I thought the obnoxiously sweet Amaretto Sour should never have left the 1970s. His grown-up version, however, changed my tune: His included double-proof whiskey to provide a boozy backbone along with the almond-y sweetness of amaretto. He used plenty of lemon juice to cut the sugar. And he served it as a flip—shaking it with egg whites, so the ice in the shaker acted like tiny whisks, whipping the egg with the sugar in the drink to create a fluffy white head that's essentially meringue. This is our version of his version, without the bourbon so it freezes the way we want it but complete with honey marshmallow creme to replicate that head, and lemon zest to evoke the lemon peel Jeffrey expressed over each cocktail.

For some boozy fun, serve the sherbet as a half-cup scoop and pour on a shot of nice bourbon at the last minute.

In the bowl of an ice cream maker, combine the sorbet base, 1 cup cold water, the milk, cream, amaretto, 1 tablespoon of the lemon zest, and the lemon juice and turn on the machine. Churn just until the mixture has the texture of a pourable frozen smoothie, 25 to 35 minutes, depending on the machine.

Meanwhile, use a spoon or flexible spatula to gently fold the remaining 1 tablespoon lemon zest into the marshmallow creme.

Once the ice cream has churned, alternate spooning layers of the ice cream and thick swirls of marshmallow creme into freezer-safe containers. Freeze until firm, at least 6 hours or for up to 3 months. (See Freezing & Storage, page 15, for tips.)

KALIMOTXO CREAM SHERBET

**MAKES ABOUT
4 PINTS**

SHERRY VANILLA ICE CREAM

3   cups 17% Butterfat
    Base (page 22)

½   cup dry Amontillado
    sherry

2   teaspoons pure
    vanilla extract,
    preferably Mexican

½   teaspoon finely grated
    orange zest (grated
    on a Microplane)

COLA SORBET

2   cups Sorbet/Sherbet
    Base (page 26)

2   cups Coca-Cola, cold

From the Basque region of Spain comes a drink that sounds like sacrilege but tastes like heaven. It's called kalimotxo, and it's one part Spanish red wine and one part Coca-Cola. We swap out red wine for its fortified, barrel-aged cousin sherry, which makes a way better showing in ice cream form. We spin a separate ice cream for each mixer and freeze them side by side in each pint to create a Creamsicle effect, then add a little orange zest to evoke the orange wedge in the classic drink.

In fact, you can use this format for other cocktails, too. For example, try subbing a nice spiced rum for the sherry (use about half the amount to accommodate the higher proof) for a Rum & Coke ice cream.

CHURN THE SHERRY ICE CREAM

In the bowl of an ice cream maker, combine the ice cream base, sherry, 1 cup cold water, the vanilla, and orange zest and turn on the machine. Churn just until the mixture has the texture of soft serve, 30 to 40 minutes, depending on the machine.

Turn your freezer-safe containers on their sides. Transfer the sherry vanilla ice cream to the containers, filling them halfway (sideways). Cover and freeze with the containers on their sides while you churn the cola sorbet (see Note).

CHURN THE COLA SORBET

In the bowl of an ice cream maker, whisk together the sorbet base and cola until combined and turn on the machine. Churn just until the mixture has the texture of a pourable frozen smoothie, 25 to 35 minutes, depending on the machine.

Transfer the sorbet to the empty sides of the containers with the sherry ice cream and freeze until firm, at least 6 hours or for up to 3 months. (See Freezing & Storage, page 15, for tips.)

NOTE · IN THIS RECIPE, YOU'RE CHURNING TWO DIFFERENT FLAVORS AND THEN COMBINING THEM IN CONTAINERS. IT'S EASY-PEASY IF YOU HAVE AN ICE CREAM MAKER CAPABLE OF MAKING MULTIPLE BATCHES WITHOUT REST, AND IT'S TOTALLY DOABLE IN A FROZEN-BOWL MACHINE, TOO. JUST TAKE A PAUSE BETWEEN CHURNING FLAVORS SO THE BOWL CAN REFREEZE FOR AT LEAST 12 HOURS PRIOR TO CHURNING THE SECOND FLAVOR.

THE RIFFS

CHAMPAGNE SORBET

MAKES ABOUT
2 PINTS

1½ cups Sorbet/Sherbet Base (page 26)

½ cup verjus or white grape juice

¼ cup freshly squeezed grapefruit juice

1 cup champagne, chilled

To make boozy ice cream, we typically go light on the alcohol, either adding it judiciously or cooking it off so the base can freeze properly. But to make this celebratory scoop, we take a tip from the world of spiked slushies. Basically, you churn sorbet, holding off on the champagne addition until those gorgeous, teeny-tiny ice crystals have developed. Only then do you add your bubbly, and somehow, though the champagne itself doesn't freeze, it gets captured in that network of ice crystals. It's fantastic on its own or floated in a little San Pellegrino aranciata.

Using quality champagne makes a huge difference here, but because it'll lose some of its nuance in sweet, icy form, I recommend using a nice dry or medium-dry sparkling wine in the $20 to $30 range. If champagne's not your thing, try this recipe with a barrel-aged sour beer, bright white wine, or chuggable effervescent red, like Lambrusco.

In a medium bowl, combine the sorbet base, verjus, ¾ cup water, and the grapefruit juice and whisk until combined.

Pour the mixture into an ice cream maker and turn on the machine. Churn just until it has the texture of a pourable frozen smoothie, 25 to 35 minutes, depending on the machine.

As soon as the sorbet reaches a smoothie texture, gradually add the chilled champagne. Let the mixture churn for another 3 minutes, stopping the sorbet while it's still a thin Slurpee consistency, before turning off the machine.

Transfer to freezer-safe containers and freeze until firm, at least 6 hours or for up to 3 months. (See Freezing & Storage, page 15, for tips.)

ACKNOWLEDGMENTS

This book was written for my two daughters, Virginia Ballantyne and Billie Day, who put up with long hours of me writing and traveling to get this book done. One day you'll be able to read this: The moment you joined our family, you taught me the meaning of undying love. Part of what I hope to give you in return is wonder. So much of what Salt & Straw does, and what I hope this book does as well, is add wonder to the world. It's more important than we recognize. The wonder we try to gift to our kids, the wonder they gift back to us.

To my wife, Sophia, who *started her own company* right in the throes of my finishing this book and somehow still found time to help me through design review and editing, while also being fully present as a parent and wife. You amaze me, and I'm so grateful to have you in my life.

To my test kitchen crew, Lauren Castagno, David Briggs, and Karla Mallari, who took on the huge challenge of the recipe testing here in Portland. Lauren, in particular, was a bulldog—an incredible, graceful bulldog!—at keeping us coordinated and on track.

This book took nearly three years to write, in part because of the sheer amount of research it required. And I couldn't have done it without the experts and friends who generously gave their time and resources. You're the greatest minds in the industry, and I'll never forget our talks and tastings. To Marty Parisien and Bill Wiedmann at Singing Dog Vanilla and to Dr. Alan Chambers at the University of Florida. To Greg D'Alesandre of Dandelion Chocolate and Sebastian Cisneros of Cocanú Chocolate.

To brothers Jerad and Justin Morrison of Sightglass Coffee. To Erika and Sebastian Degens at Stone Barn Brandyworks. To salt expert Mark Bitterman and salt maker Ben Jacobsen (of Jacobsen Salt Co.). To the late Steven Smith of Steven Smith Tea. To cereal-o-phile Emily Miller of OffLimits. And to my original mentors in dairy at Oregon State University, in particular Sarah Masoni.

To my team at Salt & Straw, especially Andee Hess, Jenny Cassel, and my cousin, Kim Malek, who stopped everything when I needed extra help with design, copy feedback, and more. Before I even started writing, Andee spent hours helping me draft the initial inspiration and design.

To the crew that technically made this possible. Thank you to immensely creative photographer Stephanie Shih, who gave up her apartment for three weeks to host our photoshoot. To our amazing crew for the shoot—Jaclyn Kershek, Ali Chiappinelli, and Jordan Dragojlovic. To cookbook superhero JJ Goode, who listens, absorbs, and tells stories in ways that no one else in the world can.

To the team at Clarkson Potter. Thank you to my editors, Francis Lam and Susan Roxborough, who helped craft this into something that I couldn't have dreamed of just a couple of years ago. To Stephanie Huntwork, Mia Johnson, and Jan Derevjanik for their creative design work and for patiently listening to my never-ending feedback. And to Darian Keels, Patricia Shaw, Kelli Tokos, Alexandra Noya, Joey Lozada, and Natalie Yera-Campbell for all your contributions to this book.

INDEX

Note: Page references in *italics* indicate photographs.

A

Acid extracts, 163
Almond Butter Fluffernutter, 190–91, *191*
Almond(s)
  Caramelized, 199
  Frangipane Cocoa Nib, *71,* 74–75
  Frangipane Swirl, 75
  Honey Rocky Road, 198–99, *200*
  Jasmine Milk Tea Straciatella, 233
  Pistachio Cream, 185
Amaretto Sour Sherbet, *244, 246*
Ancho Chocolate Cinnamon, 67
Apple
  Pie, Ritz Streusel Mock, 139
  Sherbet, Salted Caramel, 163
Apricot Meadow Marmalade, 226, *227*
Assam Tea Caramel Swirls, 225
Avocado & Strawberry Jam, 91, *91*

B

Banana(s)
  Coffee Toffee Banoffee, 118–19
  Foster Caramel, 166
  Foster Rum Caramel, 166, *172*
  Honey-Roasted, Vanilla, 39
Base recipes
  The Richest Custard Base Ever, 24
  Salt & Straw's Coveted 17% Butterfat Base, 22
  Salt & Straw's Super-Dense Gelato Base, 25
  Salt & Straw's Super-Easy Sorbet/Sherbet Base, 26
  Salt & Straw's Vegan Coconut Base, 27
Berry. *See also specific berries*
  Wild, Pie Filling, 98
  Wild-Foraged, Pie, 96–98, *97*
Birthday Cake
  & Blackberries, *44,* 45–46
  Crumble, 46
Blackberries & Birthday Cake, *44,* 45–46

Black Pepper Goat Cheese Ganache, 82, *83*
Black Sesame Marshmallows, 232
Bourbon Brown Sugar Vanilla, 38
Bourbon (aka Madagascar) vanilla, 36
Brioche, Butter-Toasted, Crumble, 190
Brittle, Thai Chile–Cashew, 202
Brown Sugar
  Bourbon Vanilla, 38
  Butterscotch Swirl, 43
  Cinnamon Goo, 116
Butterscotch
  Swirl, 43
  Swirls, Vanilla Custard with, 42–43, *43*

C

Cacao, history of, 60
Cake
  Carrot, 196
  Chocolate, Ganache-Glazed, 175
  Cinnamon Coffee, 117, *117*
  Coffee Tres Leches, 125
  Pecan Toffee Pudding, *192,* 193
  Vanilla Tres Leches, 95
Campari & Raw Rhubarb Sorbet, *244, 245*
Candy thermometer, 17
Caramel. *See also* Salted Caramel
  Assam Tea Swirls, 225
  Bananas Foster, 166
  -Chocolate Cupcakes, 171
  Chocolate Potato Chip Cupcake, *172,* 173–75
  Cinnamon-Spiced, 51
  Cocoa Nib Almond Frangipane, *71,* 74–75
  Coffee Toffee Banoffee, 118–19
  Fish Sauce, 179
  Pandan-Cilantro, 203
  Perfect Ice Cream, 119
  Swirls, Vanilla with Sticky Croissants and, 50–51
Cardamom & Coffee White Chocolate, 112, *112*
Carrot Cake, 196
Carrot Cake Pecan Praline, 194–97, *195*

Cashew
  Brittle with Pandan Cilantro Caramel, *200,* 201–3
  –Thai Chile Brittle, 202
Cashew Milk
  Coffee Chamomile Sorbet, *122,* 123
  Latte, 120
Cereal
  creative riffs, list of, 212–13
  Pots of Gold & Rainbows, *209,* 210
Chamomile
  Coffee Sorbet, *122,* 123
  Meadow Marmalade, 226, *227*
Champagne Sorbet, 248, *249*
Cheesecake, Liquid, 103
Cheesecake, Strawberry, 102–3
Cherry, Smoked-, Vanilla, 40
Cherry Blossom Gelato, 221, *223*
Chili Crisp
  Chocolate Peanut Butter Cup, 78–81
  Peanut Butter Cups, *80,* 81
Chocolate. *See also* White Chocolate
  buying, 63
  Cake, Ganache-Glazed, 175
  -Caramel Cupcakes, 171
  Caramel Potato Chip Cupcake, *172,* 173–75
  Chili Crisp Peanut Butter Cups, *80,* 81
  Chip Dough, Salted Malted, 130–33, *131*
  Chocolate Chip, 58–59, *59*
  Cookie Chunks, 146
  -Covered Potato Chips, 174, *174*
  creative riffs, list of, 57
  Cupcake, Salted, 170–71, *172*
  Earl Grey & Lemon Shortbread, *228,* 228–29
  Fudge, Extra-Dark, Passion Fruit Vanilla with, 47–49, *48*
  Fudge Sauce, Extra-Dark, 49
  Goat Cheese Ganache, 82
  Hazelnut Cookies & Cream, 145–46
  history of, 60
  Honey Almond Rocky Road, 198–99, *200*

Jasmine Milk Tea Almond
    Straciatella, 233
Malted Cookie Dough, 132
Malted Fudge, 133
Mom, 59
Salted Caramel & Peanuts
    Straciatella, 162
Salted Coffee Mocha, 113
Sesame Butter Cups, 77
Toasted Sourdough, & EVOO, 140,
    141
Tres Leches Cake, 125
Tres Leches Cake, Coffee with,
    124–25
Cilantro-Pandan Caramel, 203
Cinnamon
    Chocolate Ancho, 67
    "Cinnatopia" Coffee Cake, 116–17
    Coffee Cake, 117, 117
    Goo, 116
    -Spiced Caramel, 51
Cocoa Nib(s), 63
    Almond Frangipane, 71, 74–75
    Black Pepper Goat Cheese
        Ganache, 82, 83
    French-Pressed, & Coffee
        Sherbet, 121
Cocoa powder, 63–65
Coconut
    Base, Salt & Straw's Vegan, 27
    Cashew Brittle with Pandan
        Cilantro Caramel, 200, 201–3
    Flakes, Candied, 144
    Jam, 205
    Shortbread Cookies, 144
    Toasted, & Samoa Butter, 136,
        138
    Triple, Cream Pie with Shortbread
        Crumble, 142, 143–44
Coconut Water Strawberry
    Sherbet, 90
Coffee
    Any-, Ice Cream, 108, 109
    brewing methods, 110
    burr grinders for, 111
    creative riffs, list of, 107
Coffee Cake, Cinnamon, 117, 117
Coffee Syrup
    Cold-Brewed, 111
    Espresso-Brewed, 111
    Steamy Cream-Immersion, 111

Cola Sorbet, 248
Containers, 17
Cookie Dough
    creative riffs, list of, 129
    Malted, 132
    Peanut Butter, 149
    Salted Malted Chocolate Chip
        Dough, 130–33, 131
Cookies
    Chocolate Cookie Chunks, 146
    Coconut Shortbread, 144
    Lemon Earl Grey Shortbread, 229
Cookies & Cream, Hazelnut,
    145–46
Cream cheese
    Cinnamon Coffee Cake, 117, 117
    Liquid Cheesecake, 103
Croissant(s)
    Honey, Twice-Baked, 51
    Vanilla with Sticky, and Caramel
        Swirls, 50–51
Crumbles
    Birthday Cake, 46
    Butter-Toasted Brioche, 190
    Graham Cracker, 103
    Pecan Praline, 197
Cucumber Strawberry Sorbet,
    92, 93
Cupcakes, Chocolate-Caramel,
    171
Currants
    Brown Butter Rice Pudding, 136,
        150–51
    Verjus-Soaked, 151
Custard Base, The Richest Ever, 24

D
Date(s)
    Pecan Toffee Pudding, 192, 193
    Shake, Chocolate-Freckled, 68,
        69

E
Earl Grey
    Chocolate, & Lemon Shortbread,
        228, 228–29
    Shortbread, Lemon, 229
    Smoked Black Tea with Black
        Sesame Marshmallows,
        231–32

F
Fernet & Maple, 243
Fig & Sesame Butter Cup, 71,
    76–77
Fish Sauce Caramel &
    Lemongrass, 178–79
French Vanilla, 32–33, 33
Fudge, Malted, 133

G
Ganache, Goat Cheese, 82
Gelato
    Base, Salt & Straw's Super-
        Dense, 25
    Cherry Blossom, 221, 223
    Hazelnut Coffee, 114, 115
    Pistachio, 184–85, 185
    Sour Cream, 101
    Strawberry, 88–89, 89
    Vanilla Poached Peach, 53
Genmai
    Brown Butter Rice Pudding, 136,
        150–51
    Roasted Strawberries with
        Japanese Whiskey, 99
Goat Cheese
    Black Pepper Ganache, 82, 83
    Ganache, 82
Graham Cracker
    Coffee Toffee Banoffee, 118–19
    Crumble, 103
Grapefruit
    Champagne Sorbet, 248, 249
    Salted Caramelized, Sherbet, 176
Green tea
    creative riffs, list of, 217
    Matcha Matcha Man, 218, 219

H
Hazelnut
    Coffee Gelato, 114, 115
    Cookies & Cream, 145–46
    Praline, 188, 189
    Pralines & Cream, 188
Hibiscus
    Big Hibiscicle, 222, 223
Honey
    Almond Rocky Road, 198–99, 200
    Croissants, Twice-Baked, 51
    Marshmallow Creme, 199
    -Roasted Banana Vanilla, 39

Honeycomb Candy, Salted Sweet
  Cream with, 167–68

I
Ice cream
  freezing and storing, 15
  history and evolution of, 240
  serving, 16
Ice cream machines, 14

J
Jam, Coconut, 205
Jasmine Milk Tea Almond
  Straciatella, 233

K
Kalimotxo Cream Sherbet, *244*,
  247

L
Lapsang souchong
  Smoked Black Tea with Black
    Sesame Marshmallows,
    231–32
  Smoked-Cherry Vanilla, 40
Lemon
  Earl Grey Shortbread, 229
  Zest & Salted Meringues, *136*,
    137
Lemongrass & Fish Sauce
  Caramel, 178–79

M
Macadamia
  Nuts, Candied, 205
  Toasted, with Coconut Jam,
    204–5
Malted Cookie Dough, 132
Malted Fudge, 133
Maple & Fernet, 243
Marmalade, Meadow, 226, *227*
Marshmallow Creme, 191
  Almond Butter Fluffernutter,
    190–91, *191*
  Amaretto Sour Sherbet, *244*, 246
  Chili Crisp Chocolate Peanut
    Butter Cup, 78–81
  Honey, 199
  Honey Almond Rocky Road,
    198–99, *200*
  Triple Coconut Cream Pie with
    Shortbread Crumble, *142*,
    143–44

Marshmallows
  Black Sesame, 232
  Brown-Butter Pepitas, 151
Matcha Matcha Man, 218, *219*
Meringues, Vanilla, & Lemon Zest,
  136, 137
Mexican vanilla, 36
Mint Chocolate Chip, Freckled,
  72, 73
Mocha, Salted Coffee, 113

N
Nuts. *See also specific nuts*
  about, 186
  fresh, buying, 186

P
Pandan-Cilantro Caramel, 203
Parchment paper, 17
Passion Fruit Vanilla with Extra-
  Dark Chocolate Fudge, 47–49,
  48
Peach, Vanilla Poached, Gelato, 53
Peanut Butter
  Cookie Dough, 149
  Cup, Chili Crisp Chocolate, 78–81
  Cups, Chili Crisp, *80*, 81
  & Jelly Cookie Dough, 148–49
  –Salted Chocolate, 66
Peanuts & Salted Caramel
  Straciatella, 162
Pecan
  Praline, Carrot Cake, 194–97, *195*
  Praline Crumble, 197
  Sticky Toffee Pudding, 192–93
  Toffee Pudding, *192*, 193
Pepitas
  Brown-Butter, 151
  Brown Butter Rice Pudding, *136*,
    150–51
Pineapple
  Caramelized, Sherbet, 164, *165*
  Carrot Cake, 196
  Cashew Brittle with Pandan
    Cilantro Caramel, *200*, 201–3
Pistachio
  Cream, 185
  creative riffs, list of, 183
  Gelato, 184–85, *185*
Potato Chip Cupcake, Chocolate
  Caramel, *172*, 173–75
Potato Chips, Chocolate-Covered,
  174, *174*

Pots of Gold & Rainbows, *209*, 210
Praline
  Hazelnut, 188, *189*
  Pecan, Crumble, 197
Pretzel, Salted, Ice Cream, 134
Pudding, Pecan Toffee, *192*, 193
Puff Pastry Crust Chunks, 98

R
Raisin(s). *See* Rum Raisin(s)
Raspberry(ies)
  Cherry Blossom Gelato, 221, *223*
  Peanut Butter & Jelly Cookie
    Dough, 148–49
  Rosé Frozé, 242, *242*
  Rhubarb, Raw, & Campari Sorbet,
    244, 245
Rice Pudding, Brown Butter, *136*,
  150–51
Ritz Streusel Mock Apple Pie, 139
Rocky Road, Almond Honey,
  198–99, *200*
Rosé Frozé, 242, *242*
Rum Caramel, Bananas Foster,
  166, *172*
Rum Raisin(s)
  Candied, 239
  creative riffs, list of, 237
  Custard, 238–39, *239*
  Syrup, 239

S
Salt, 17, 160–61
Salted Caramel, 156–59, *157*
  about, 158
  creative riffs, list of, 155
  Syrup, 159
Samoa Butter & Toasted Coconut,
  136, 138
Sauce, Extra-Dark Chocolate
  Fudge, 49
Scotch
  Butterscotch Swirl, 43
Sesame Butter Cup & Fig, *71*,
  76–77
Sesame Butter Cups, 77
Sherbet. *See also* Sorbet/Sherbet
  Caramelized Pineapple, 164, *165*
  Strawberry Coconut Water, 90
  Toasted Milk, Assam Tea
    Caramel, *223*, 224–25
Sherry Vanilla Ice Cream, 247

Shortbread
  Cookies, Coconut, 144
  Crumble, Triple Coconut Cream
    Pie with, *142,* 143–44
  Lemon Earl Grey, 229
Silicone baking mat, 17
Smoked-Cherry Vanilla, 40
Sorbet/Sherbet
  Amaretto Sour Sherbet, *244, 246*
  Base, Salt & Straw's Super-Easy,
    26
  Big Hibiscicle, 222, *223*
  Cashew Milk Latte, 120
  Chocolate Sorbet, 70, *71*
  Coffee Chamomile Sorbet, *122,*
    123
  Cola Sorbet, 248
  Fernet & Maple, 243
  French-Pressed Cocoa Nibs &
    Coffee Sherbet, 121
  Raw Rhubarb & Campari Sorbet,
    244, 245
  Rosé Frozé, 242, *242*
  Salted Caramel Apple Sherbet,
    163
  Salted Caramelized Grapefruit
    Sherbet, 176
  Strawberry Cucumber Sorbet,
    92, *93*
Sour Cream
  Gelato, 101
  Liquid Cheesecake, 103
  & Strawberries, *100,* 101
Sourdough, Toasted, Chocolate &
  EVOO, 140, *141*
Stick blender, 17
Strawberry
  creative riffs, list of, 87
  Gelato, 88–89, *89*

Syrups
  Cold-Brewed Coffee, 111
  Espresso-Brewed Coffee, 111
  Rum Raisin, 239
  Salted Caramel, 159
  Steamy Cream-Immersion
    Coffee, 111

T
Tahini
  Sesame Butter Cups, 77
Tahitian vanilla, 36
Tea makers, 220
Thai Chile–Cashew Brittle, 202
Toasted Milk Sherbet Assam Tea
  Caramel, *223,* 224–25
Tres Leches
  Cake, Chocolate, 125
  Cake, Vanilla, 95
  Strawberry, 94–95

V
Vanilla
  buying, 35–36
  creative riffs, list of, 31
  extract, about, 35–36
  French, 32–33, *33*
  growing and harvesting, 34–35
  history of, 34
  specks, about, 36
  Tres Leches Cake, 95
Vegan recipes
  Bananas Foster Rum Caramel,
    166, *172*
  Caramelized Pineapple Sherbet,
    164, *165*
  Cashew Brittle with Pandan
    Cilantro Caramel, *200,* 201–3
  Cashew Milk Latte, 120
  Champagne Sorbet, 248, *249*

Chocolate Sorbet, 70, *71*
Coffee Chamomile Sorbet, *122,*
  123
Freckled Mint Chocolate Chip,
  72, 73
Hazelnut Cookies & Cream,
  145–46
Passion Fruit Vanilla with Extra-
  Dark Chocolate Fudge, 47–49,
  48
Rosé Frozé, 242, *242*
Salt & Straw's Vegan Coconut
  Base, 27
Strawberry Coconut Water
  Sherbet, 90
Strawberry Cucumber Sorbet,
  92, *93*
Verjus
  Champagne Sorbet, 248, *249*
  -Soaked Currants, 151

W
Walnut Oil Ice Cream, 187
Whiskey
  Bourbon Brown Sugar Vanilla, 38
  Butterscotch Swirl, 43
  Japanese, Roasted Strawberries
    with, 99
White Chocolate
  about, 63
  Caramelized, Vanilla with, 38
  Coffee & Cardamom, 112, *112*
Wine
  Champagne Sorbet, 248, *249*
  Rosé Frozé, 242, *242*
  Verjus-Soaked Currants, 151

X
Xanthan gum, about, 22

Published in the United States by
Clarkson Potter/Publishers, an
imprint of the Crown Publishing
Group, a division of Penguin
Random House LLC, New York.
ClarksonPotter.com

CLARKSON POTTER is a trademark
and POTTER with colophon is a
registered trademark of Penguin
Random House LLC.

Library of Congress Cataloging-in-
Publication Data
Names: Malek, Tyler, author.
  | Goode, JJ, author. | Shih,
  Stephanie, photographer.
Title: America's most iconic ice
  creams / Tyler Malek and
  JJ Goode ; photographs by
  Stephanie Shih.
Identifiers: LCCN 2024022293
  (print) | LCCN 2024022294
  (ebook) | ISBN 9780593582107
  (hardcover) | ISBN
  9780593582114 (ebook)
Subjects: LCSH: Ice cream, ices,
  etc.—United States. | LCGFT:
  Cookbooks.
Classification: LCC TX795
  .M248 2025 (print) | LCC TX795
  (ebook) | DDC 641.86/2—dc23/
  eng/20240517
LC record available at https://lccn.
  loc.gov/2024022293
LC ebook record available at https://
  lccn.loc.gov/2024022294

ISBN 978-0-593-58210-7
Ebook ISBN 978-0-593-58211-4

Printed in China

Additional photo credits
Masking tape images (cover and
interior): WR7/Shutterstock.com
Cream-colored paper (cover and
interior, behind Notes): Asya
Alexandrova/Shutterstock.com
Picture frames (cover and interior):
joesayhello/Shutterstock.com
Hand (front cover): Luis Molinero/
Shutterstock.com
Food photos on cover: Stephanie Shih

Editors: Francis Lam
and Susan Roxborough
Editorial assistant: Darian Keels
Art director: Stephanie Huntwork
Designer: Mia Johnson
Design assistance: Jan Derevjanik
Production editor: Patricia Shaw
Production manager: Kelli Tokos
Compositors: Merri Ann Morrell
and Hannah Hunt
Food stylist: Ali Chiappinelli
Prop stylist: Jaclyn Kershek
Photo assistant: Jordan Dragojlovic
Copy editor: Sasha Tropp
Proofreaders: Lisa Lawley, Robin
Slutzky, and Sigi Nacson
Indexer: Elizabeth T. Parson
Publicist: Joey Lozada
Marketer: Natalie Yera-Campbell

10 9 8 7 6 5 4 3 2 1

First Edition